Power from Above for Turmoil Below

A Verse-by-Verse Exploration of Second Corinthians

William J. Sturm

sermonto**book**
.com

This work is dedicated to the love of my life, Nikki.

I am furthermore indebted to those who have funded this work.

CONTENTS

Why Yet Another Commentary on 2 Corinthians

Trust me, I know. I've purchased numerous commentaries myself in both hardcopy and digital formats (Logos and Kindle, primarily). This commentary is nothing short of a labor of love (Hebrews 6:10) for the people God has entrusted to me at Sandy Ridge Baptist Church of Hickory, North Carolina. They will never know my yearning for them in Christ (Galatians 4:19). They are hardworking people with love for their pastor and his family. I am humbled to be their pastor, and I desire that they would have my notes for reference in years to come when they are reading their own Bibles or citing something they supernaturally remember from the series of sermons behind these notes.

This is also a labor of love for my Lord. It seems when a man spends ten to fifteen hours a week preparing sermons and lessons and devotionals that he would like something to show for it. I simply want my messages to keep living.

In my spare time, I read for hours to supplement my preaching and understanding of the Scriptures. SRBC is "the ground and pillar of truth" (1 Timothy 3:15), and I am a gift to her (Ephesians 4:11–12). It seems, then, that I should be finding ways to re-preach these thoughts from God through His Word and through the unique personality that makes up Bill Sturm.

A word about the appendices: You can enjoy the reference-like nature of this commentary without even looking at the last sections of the book. They are more topically driven, rather than being organized for reference. I just wanted to take the opportunity this book presented to raise some eyebrows about certain topics that would otherwise have to wait for another commentary.

May God alone be glorified, and may His church receive the credit for allowing Him to be so.

—*William J. Sturm*

CHAPTER ONE

"Fellow Workers": 2 Corinthians 1

1:1–4

Paul, an apostle of Jesus Christ by the will of God, and Timothy _our_ brother, To the church of God which is at Corinth, with all the saints who are in all Achaia: 2 Grace to you and peace from God our Father and the Lord Jesus Christ. 3 Blessed _be_ the God and Father of our Lord Jesus Christ, the Father of mercies and God of all comfort,

Right away, we need to know that the word comfort is used in each of the next four verses as well, and it shows up again in chapters 7 and 8. So we know that the reason Paul is taking the time to tell these folks about the God they are serving is because, quite simply, he is going to talk to them about how their theology drives their philosophy, or how their view of God drives their view of life. The other three seeming descriptions of God—"grace," "peace," and "mercies"—are apparently not on Paul's

6 · WILLIAM J. STURM

plate. He wants you to know something about God's comfort.

4 who comforts us in all our tribulation,
Perhaps this is the right time to say this carries the idea of a cheering and supporting influence.

that we may be able to comfort those who are in any trouble, with the comfort with which we ourselves are comforted by God.
We cannot give strength where we have found none. We do not have any power to give advice if we do not first have a measure of wisdom—at least not advice worth hearing. So it is in the emotional part of men and women: We must have some measure of comfort that comes only from God if we expect to help others find such a comfort.

1:5
For as the sufferings
Here again is a word that occurs in the next two verses as well.

of Christ abound in us, so our consolation also abounds through Christ.[1]
Our comfort that allows us to convey emotional stability to others is found only in concert with sufferings we suffer with Christ. It's true, and we find our comfort from Him. What's the math here? Well, if we suffer the death of Christ in our daily lives, then we can most certainly find

---

[1] Here it would do well to remind us of Philippians 3:10 and Paul's motive behind his desire.

gospel-centered assurance that the Father of mercies will exonerate us, His servants.

One more thing: you may notice that Paul sort of tells us that the consolation or comfort is in proportion to the suffering, for he uses the word "abound" in both aspects. Other translations do a fine job of drawing this out when it speaks of the group traveling with Paul as having abundant suffering.

1:6
Now if we are afflicted, *it is* for your consolation and salvation, which is effective
The word used for "it is" is a middle voice participle which means that the salvation was working upon itself (the Greek is the word from which we get "energy") as the Corinthians were enduring. This salvation was actually energizing the Corinthian church's endurance of the same sufferings. As they would see, they would feel. As they would feel, they would walk on.

for enduring the same sufferings which we also suffer. Or if we are comforted, it is for your consolation and salvation.
Whatever extremes we experience—good or bad—are for the comfort and salvaging of people everywhere. They are to experience salvaging or salvation and comfort. The question remains: salvation from what? From sin and Hell? From sin as a believer? From tribulation?

Let's read on…

1:7

And our hope for you *is* **steadfast,**

The ESV says "unshaken."

because we know that as you are partakers of the sufferings, so also *you will partake* **of the consolation.**
There is a reasonable assurance that all those who are suffering for Christ will actually find comfort in their great difficulty. Now, you cannot imagine this, but Paul is saying, "Your confidence is shaken. You're feeling pressed down, but our confidence (verse 7) is unshaken."

You may feel unfit for the life ahead of you, but you need to know straightaway that you seem to be a believer because of your enduring faith, and some of us who have seen the end of this idea know that you will partake in his consolation.

1:8–9

For we do not want you to be ignorant, brethren, of our trouble which came to us in Asia: that we were burdened beyond measure,
There is no way to express how much weight they felt. It was absolutely unbearable.

above strength,
Or, probably, the "sufferings … in abundance" of verse 5 (NASB).

so that we despaired even of life. 9 Yes, we had the sentence of death in ourselves [we were walking dead],

that we should not trust in ourselves but in God who raises the dead,
This reality of sure comfort does not always arrive immediately. Rather, there are desperate times when dreading one's life is a real part of the difficulty that arises in the sufferer's life. There are those who find comfort only in desperate faith—a desperate faith that believes the God who saved them from death and Hell will yet do it again. He really is "the One who lifts up my head" (Psalm 3:3 NKJV).

We see, then, the connection between Christ's deliverance from death and our own. He was raised from the dead by God, and we are told at least a practical connection between Christ's sufferings and ours— Christ's death and our experiential death. Simply put, if you look at the gospel, you will see the utter terror of suffering, the utter hopelessness of burial, and the shocking power of a God who can and does rescue from death. So, do you feel the cold hand of death?

1:10
who delivered us from so great a death, and does deliver us; in whom we trust that He will still deliver *us,*
Paul takes this fifth point a little further when he speaks of three stages of deliverance—all of which are related to "trust" (verse 9). If God can be trusted for salvation, He can be trusted now. We know there will be a time, ultimately, when we will be saved. We trust for the future. We trust Him for the past. Now, then, in this great suffering, we find consolation for the present. We trust that He is yet delivering us. How? I don't know, but if you would

have looked at Paul, you would have seen what he did not see. You could have told him, "While you are dying, Paul, we are finding life."

1:11
you also helping together in prayer for us,

> Romans 15:30-31 Now I beg you, brethren, through the Lord Jesus Christ, and through the love of the Spirit, that you **strive together with me in prayers** to God for me, 31 that I may be delivered from those in Judea who do not believe, and that my service for Jerusalem may be acceptable to the saints....

> Philippians 1:15-19 Some indeed preach Christ even from envy and strife, and some also from goodwill: 16 The former preach Christ from selfish ambition, not sincerely, supposing to add affliction to my chains; 17 but the latter out of love, knowing that I am appointed for the defense of the gospel. 18 What then? Only that in every way, whether in pretense or in truth, Christ is preached; and in this I rejoice, yes, and will rejoice. 19 For I know that **this will turn out for my deliverance through your prayer** and the supply of the Spirit of Jesus Christ....

> Philemon 1:22 But, meanwhile, also prepare a guest room for me, for I trust that **through your prayers** I shall be granted to you.

that thanks may be given by many persons on our behalf for the gift granted to us through many.
Our prayers are multi-generational in their impact. Many persons will be thanking God for us and the grace of God we bring to them, which is possible, in part, because of

your prayers. This is pretty special coming from a guy who says, "I labored more abundantly than they all" (1 Corinthians 15:10 NKJV). Your prayers are accomplishing amazing things in the hearts of those you may never meet because you pray for those who are impacting them.

I ask you again: how did Paul know that they were praying for him? He must have sensed remarkable enablement and profound differences for him to say, "We know you've been helping in prayer for us!" Imagine the wonderment of knowing that people are praying for you specifically. Paul was not counting on people floating generalities up to the sky. That is not what is being communicated here.

1:12
For our boasting is this: the testimony of our conscience that we conducted ourselves in the world in simplicity
They had a clean conscience. Let me give you a sign that you or I may not have a crystal-clear conscience: we go around seeking justification from others for our actions. We don't let the Lord approve of us in our spirits. We have a smugness, an unrest, or a moodiness that screams for approval from everyone but the Lord. You know how this is. We mask it with telling everybody about what we've done or what we've said, but deep down inside we are hoping, first of all, that they will approve and, second of all, that their approval will help us feel a little better.

"Simplicity" has the idea of not being duplicitous in one's lifestyle. Consider it as the opposite of complex.

Paul and Timothy lived their lives in such a way that people didn't have to say, "Well, let's wait a month and see if this changes. Maybe they're just acting like the new preachers in town. Let's see if they still love us and visit us and preach to us when the honeymoon wears off."

and godly sincerity,
This is not that "without wax" meaning of "sincerity" we find in Philippians 1:10. This is a different Greek word altogether. This has the idea of "clear" or "ingenuousness" (as opposed to being disingenuous). But we are really helped with the adjective "godly." Paul was so clear and clean that he reflected the Heavenly Father. This, along with that non-duplicitous life, helps you see that you are not going to meet Pastor A today and Pastor B tomorrow.

not with fleshly wisdom but by the grace of God, and more abundantly toward you.
There were times when Paul and his companions motivated churches to do things differently from "Corporate" Rome. "We didn't run our business meetings the way the ungodly do. We didn't always run things in the budget committees the way Congress does. We didn't always see an immediate return for all that we did for souls."

1:13–14
For we are not writing any other things to you than what you read or understand. Now I trust you will understand, even to the end 14 (as also you have understood us in part),

We use easy-to-understand terminology that reflects that we understand a level of urgency. Take a quick look ahead at 3:12 and see how Paul was not going to let these believers off the hook of thinking things through. He is furthermore saying, "This little note I've sent you here requires your full attention, just as you have gotten ours."

In the grander context, now, we see that Paul is saying, "You're not allowed just to sit back and let the Lord massage your heartaches (verses 5–8). No, you are to understand that you have an intellectual and emotional obligation with this letter you are about to read."

that we are your boast as you also *are* ours, in the day of the Lord Jesus.
Paul is referring to that time described in his earlier letter to them (1 Corinthians 1:7–8, 5:5).

1. We suffer together (2 Corinthians 1:5–8).
2. We pray together (2 Corinthians 1:11).
3. We celebrate together (2 Corinthians 1:14). We talk about how we never would have made it through (2 Corinthians 1:8) if it had not been for you. Another party would say, "We never would have been brought strength and encouragement had it not been for you." Nobody in Heaven is saying, "Look what I've done!"

Mutual "boasting" around the throne: Each will be thanking the other.

1:15–18

**And in this confidence I intended to come to you be-
fore, that you might have a second benefit—16 to pass
by way of you to Macedonia, to come again from Macedonia to you,[2] and be helped by you on my way to
Judea. 17 Therefore, when I was planning this, did I
do it lightly? Or the things I plan, do I plan according
to the flesh, that with me there should be Yes, Yes, and
No, No? 18 But *as* God *is* faithful, our word to you was
not Yes and No.**

Basically, we see that Paul is making a connection between his preaching and his plans: "I told you I have been
wanting to come, and I didn't."[3] What changed his mind?
Well, this letter says that his original plans would have
made the Corinthian church sorry. They would have heard
(2 Corinthians 1:8) about the trouble that Paul experienced between these two verses, seen a worn-out apostle,
and possibly received the correction they were about to
receive in 2 Corinthians 2:5 as the ramblings of a tired old
man. First Corinthians 4:9 bears this out as well. Paul intended to visit this church on his third missionary journey,
but he didn't.[4]

Paul, in 2 Corinthians 3:2–3, is careful to tell these believers that they are actually walking, breathing Bibles,
and he admits here that our conduct can also teach bad
theology.

---

[2] 1 Corinthians 16:3–6
[3] When one reads Acts 19:21, it looks as though Paul wanted to go
through Achaia, yet we find a change of plans in Acts 20:3.
[4] The church begun on his second journey in Acts 18.

1:19

For the Son of God, Jesus Christ, who was preached among you by us—by me, Silvanus, and Timothy— was not Yes and No, but in Him was Yes.

This is why we don't lie to our children. If we are not serious about the omnipresent Santa, then what about a God with the same traits? If you don't keep your word about ball games and commitments to relationships, what should other people believe about the God you serve?

Christ's character drives me to be honest. We ought to be people who give unmingled signals.

1:20–21

For all the promises of God in Him *are* Yes, and in Him Amen, to the glory of God through us. 21 Now He who establishes us with you in Christ and has anointed us *is* God,

We all know about those who are busy explaining themselves. Instead, we need to reassure those around us of the truth to which we adhere by emphasizing what is true of God and by placing us all on equal ground ("it's true for you and me").

1:22–23

who also has sealed[5] us and given us the Spirit in our hearts as a guarantee.

Paul points out that we are equally marked by God for later possession.

---

[5] This is found in Ephesians 1 and Ephesians 4 and may be alluded to in 2 Timothy 2:19.

23 Moreover I call God as witness against my soul, that to spare you I came no more to Corinth.
Sometimes you just need to reaffirm your purpose with people so they think better of your intentions.

1:24
Not that we have dominion over your faith, but are fellow workers for your joy; for by faith you stand.
Paul says he and the Corinthians are equally "standing."

CHAPTER TWO

Sorrow, Love, and Triumph: 2 Corinthians 2

2:1–2

But I determined this within myself, that I would not come again to you in sorrow. 2 For if I make you sorrowful, then who is he who makes me glad but the one who is made sorrowful by me?

Paul was enduring hardship for benefit outside himself.

2:3-4[6]

2:5

But if anyone has caused grief, he has not grieved me, but all of you to some extent - not to be too severe.

Here Paul is referencing the third letter to the Corinthians (2 Corinthians 2:3–4). He is referencing this issue of guilt

---

[6] 2 Corinthians 8:22; Galatians 5:10; 2 Thessalonians 3:4; Philemon 1:21—how was all this possible? Paul gave people up to the grace of God.

by association with a man who is misbehaving in the church. His first letter, which we do not have but is referenced in 1 Corinthians, gives the principle of separating yourself from so-called believers who do not live a consistent life. His second letter (which we call "First Corinthians") points out a particular man who fit that description—he was misbehaving with a woman. His third letter (which we do not have) is referenced in 2 Corinthians 2:3–4 and prescribes forgiveness of the man he was trying to get them to punish in "First Corinthians." This fourth letter (which we call "Second Corinthians") gives them a particular reminder of forgiveness and an additional errand of reaffirming their love as found in verse 8.

We find in verses 12 through 13 that Titus was the mailman of this third letter (which we do not have), and Paul writes about the anxiety he experienced while he awaited Titus's report. He was aching to ask him, "How did the church in Corinth respond to my note?" In fact, he was so worried that he left a preaching opportunity to "intersect Titus" on his way back from Corinth.[7] That, friends, is how any preacher worth his salt deals with hard errands of telling you truth. He quakes and loves and preaches and loves and waits for your response.

6 This punishment which was inflicted by the majority is sufficient [or adequate] **for such a man,**
This majority punishment was "**sufficient**." Paul is saying, "You did a good job. Now...."

---

[7] John MacArthur, ed., *Macarthur Study Bible (NKJV)* (_____: Thomas Nelson Bibles, 1997), 1766.

Imagine how awkward this gets with some three- and four-generation families at our churches. This is another reason why we should pay attention. We don't ever want to face a situation where family members are forced to take part in adequate punishment against their family member.

2:7

so that, on the contrary, you ought rather to forgive and comfort him, lest perhaps such a one be swallowed up with too much sorrow.

Let us allow the context from verse 3 to drive this train: "You, as a church, have a problem forgiving somebody." Now, let us understand that we are not about to get into a willy-nilly forgiveness where you just let everyone off on everything. However, we do want to understand the reason Paul couldn't come and be encouraged by this particular church was because if he came and corrected them, it would ruin the spirit of the visit (and thus, his third letter asking them to forgive). The real issue is that Paul needed to be refreshed. Take a look again at 2 Corinthians 1:8 and 2 Corinthians 2:3–4 and see that the spiritual health Paul needed was not possible, and that consequently caused him deep grief (2 Corinthians 2:3–4).

2:8

Therefore I urge you to reaffirm *your* love to him.

Paul is saying, "Convince him of your love for him in proportion to the conviction with which you persuaded him of his wrong. Be just as tenacious in your loving him as you were in your vehemence against his sin when you put

him out." This was a normal trait of the Corinthians.
When they knew they were wrong about something, they
quickly and profoundly dealt with it! They even answered
well in accordance with the letter Paul had sent telling
them to forgive (see 2 Corinthians 7:8–12).

Now, as mentioned previously, he is asking them to
take their forgiveness a little further and to swallow up a
man with love who is otherwise swallowed up with his
own sorrow. We are to go from relatively passive forgiveness to rather active love. Remember, we are not
talking about people who don't belong in your church because of outward, unrepentant rebellious behavior. Paul
isn't asking that.

2:9
For to this end I also wrote,
The Holman leaves out "also." Paul is saying, "Here's
why I wrote...."

**that I might put you to the test, whether you are obe-
dient in all things.**
Second Corinthians 7:12 makes it pretty clear that this was
for their benefit, not his. Forgiveness is primarily for the
person who forgives. Don't forget that, as Anthony Starr,
Deacon Chairman at SRBC, put it, "Being unforgiving is
like drinking poison and expecting somebody else to die."

We find out that the very reason Paul chose not to come
was for the errand itself. He did not want to dampen the
spirit of the visit by correcting them in person. Think of

it, an apostle changed his travel plans (late chapter 1) because of the unforgiving spirit the church was exercising toward one man!

How is this possible? One possibility is that the church met in a family's home. First Corinthians 1:11–16 mentions the household of Chloe and the household of Stephanas. What if the church met in one of these homes? The man who was otherwise unforgiven was not allowed into a home for worship and fellowship.

Now, was what they did wrong? Was it wrong for them to put a man out of their fellowship? Notice again: "I might put you to the test, whether you are obedient in all things" (2 Corinthians 2:9 NKJV). The word "all" is important. It should raise a question mark inside of you. Why was Paul using this quantitative word? One idea is that Paul had previously told them to obey him in another action he required of them. I think we know what this action from the past was. Review 1 Corinthians 5 for the issue.

2:10
Now whom you forgive anything, I also forgive. For if indeed I have forgiven anything, I have forgiven that one for your sakes in the presence of Christ,
Again, this is a great hint that we are talking about 1 Corinthians 5:3, where Paul writes, "For I indeed, as absent in body but present in spirit, have already judged [as though I were present] him who has so done this deed" (NKJV). He was not even there, and he had already made up his mind. Here he is saying, "Just like you sent this man packing without me, you can forgive him without me. Just

like you sent him out on my behalf, so you can receive
him back on my behalf."

2:11
**lest Satan should take advantage of us; for we are not
ignorant of his devices.**
We are not new to the idea of sneaky, harmful things
creeping into the Christian's world through repackaging
and desensitizing—for example, vampire books, depress-
ing music, and questionable apparel for the believer.[8]
We've always known that those influences from pop culture could hurt us, but is this really saying that Satan can
take advantage of us?

Perhaps the Corinthians wondered, "Aren't we doing
something that was God's idea? Aren't we doing something His apostle told us to do?" Yes, but as we realize,
doing the right thing in the wrong spirit can be demonic.
We are fully aware that others can be used by Satan (2
Corinthians 10:4–5; Ephesians 6:12), but how often do we
see ourselves as tools of Satan in the lives of others? How
often do we see ourselves bringing disadvantage to the
people of God, to the church of God, to the individual
child of God through our own sin?

Even more specifically, lover of Christ, how often do
we view our lack of forgiveness as Satan's work? See in
1 Corinthians 5 that the discipline of the church member
was not for the comfort of the church but for the correction
of the so-called convert. That's the point. They were to
put out the person who was acting unconverted and see if

---

[8] http://www.sermonaudio.com/sermon-
info.asp?SID=112012959215

he felt left out. It is implied through his brokenness that he did feel left out. He repented and wanted back in. Then Paul urged the Corinthians to forgive him.

Take note of the second part of the verse: "for we are not ignorant of his devices" (2 Corinthians 2:11 KJV). We look at feuding children and say, "We don't do that;" we want our children to live up to an ideal behavior. We really mean, "You are doing that, but I don't want you doing that." So also, Paul—using God's pen—says, "We are acting like we don't know what Satan's doing, but we need not live this way."

2:14
Now thanks be unto God, which always causeth us to triumph in Christ, [leading us in conquering procession] (as seen in the ESV, NRSV, and HCSB)

> The image of participation in a divinely led triumphal procession stems from the parading of victorious Roman generals through the streets of Rome with captives trailing behind and incense perfuming the air in thanks to the gods.[9]

Even Zedekiah, taken back toward Babylon, experienced being paraded behind the Babylonian victory march.

Here Paul is saying that as he journeyed back to hear Titus's report (this takes place in Acts 20:5), it was an

---

[9] Gordon D. Fee and Robert L. Hubbard Jr., eds., *The Eerdmans Companion to the Bible* (Grand Rapids, MI; Cambridge, U.K.: William B. Eerdmans Publishing Company, 2011), 662.

anxious walk, not seeing Titus. It was an anxious walk, wanting to know if the Corinthian believers still loved him after his third letter requiring that forgiveness. It was a desperate, life-sucking walk because he needed refreshment, but—as we learned in chapter 1—he changed his plans so as not to bring a heaviness to the Corinthians again; he consequently did without that personal dialogue that he needed so badly. Paul was furthermore passing on an open door to speak. He was passing on a great revival and a great conference and a great crusade. He was doing without an open door and a grand harvest. It was a heavy, defeating, desperate walk. In the middle of that, Paul said, "My heavy-hearted travel was a victory parade."

Were you passed over for a job? Keep walking, desperate in trust to your God, for He is leading you on a victory parade that will end on the horizons of Heaven. Were you underappreciated in your selection for a team? Keep walking, keep plodding, keep stepping on your journey, desperately committing yourself to the One who is leading you in triumph. Are you feeling dry? Are you feeling depleted? Are you feeling isolated from loved ones through no faults of your own? Keep pulling your plow in that victory march, and you'll feel, as I have felt and others around you have felt, your steps getting a little lighter. Here Paul, full of faith, says to you, "I'm feeling led by a King immortal, invisible, and the only wise God." Hear him say, "God has lavished us with riches in Christ which drive us to victory."

and through us, diffuses the fragrance of His knowledge in every place.

You are meant to smell of God and Christ in this world so the whole place will know Him. Take a look at verses 15 and 16.

2:15–16
15 For we are to God the fragrance of Christ among those who are being saved and among those who are perishing. 16 To the one we are the aroma of death leading to death, and to the other the aroma of life leading to life. And who is sufficient for these things? 17 For we are not, as so many, peddling the word of God; but as of sincerity, but as from God, we speak in the sight of God in Christ.

Our sacrifice is pleasing to God on both counts: the death odor of the lost and the lively odor of the saved.

In all ways, in every place, we are under the scope. The world is watching as Christ escorts us through life in victory—victory in heaviness. Some watch the parade and smell the death of the old selves as they have shared in our salvation. They desire our salvation. They smell our victory savor and watch our victory parade, and what do they do? They salivate for our deliverance. They smell the death of the old man.

Others fear us, and they know not why. They see our ticker-tape, heavenly displays, and they cower in dismay. They don't know how we won, but they don't like that we win. They don't understand us, but it is easier for them to assume that we are doing it through sorcery or mental technique. They smell the impending death of their own souls. The gospel, however, never ceases in its pleasing aroma to God, says Chrysostom:

The light, even when it blinds someone, is still light. Honey, though it is bitter to those who are sick, is still sweet. So also the gospel has a sweet savor to all, even those who do not believe it are lost.[10]

"And who *is* sufficient [the word "adequate" appears in the NASB (95 update)] for these things?"

One only needs to glance at 2 Corinthians 2:17 through 3:5 to see what Paul felt was his main way of shining or, better yet, of smelling—his way of giving off his victory stench. How can we know that Paul was being led in a victory procession? He was still preaching. Paul was on his journey, and we find it was his custom to minister as he traveled. Preaching was a matter of ministry for Paul, and he felt the weight of turning people "on" or "off" by the very same preaching!

Please notice that preaching or teaching the Bible was not one of the things he had to offer. It was, rather, the totality of what he did, and it caused death.

Preaching:

1. Paul kept saying that was his main mission (1 Corinthians 1:17, 2:2, 15:10).
2. He was arguably not good at it (1 Corinthians 2:3–5). Although he was not good at it from the perspective of the mechanics or technique of preaching, he had something far more satisfying: a clean testimony (2 Corinthians 2:17) and the fruit

---

[10] Thomas C. Oden, ed. *Ancient Christian Commentary on Scripture (NT: Volume VII)* (Downers Grove: Intervarsity Press, 1999), 210.

of his listener's lives (which he eluded to in 1 Corinthians 4:10 but came back to in this epistle, 2
Corinthians 3:1–4).

3. Paul did other things in the ministry (2 Corinthians
12:15).

4. Paul knew that with preaching at these open doors
comes great adversity (1 Corinthians 16:9).

CHAPTER THREE

"The Glory That Excels": 2 Corinthians 3

3: 4–6

4 And we have such trust through Christ toward God. 5 Not that we are sufficient of ourselves to think of anything as being from ourselves, but our sufficiency *is* from God, 6 who also made us sufficient as ministers of the new covenant, not of the letter but of the Spirit; for the letter kills, but the Spirit gives life.

Paul is, again, speaking about his, Timothy's, and Titus's effectiveness as ministers. Now we are going to see that Paul is building off of the living letter premise of 2 Corinthians 2:17–3:4.[11]

---

[11] Don't forget now, Paul's endurance and adequacy were wrapped up in how Christ had brought him victoriously out of anguish and difficult times so that he could do what God called him to do. We could say, "Paul was depressed," and that Paul did the will of God in his life. On the other side of it, he could say that some were saved to God's glory and others were lost to God's glory as they beheld that victory parade we discussed in the previous chapter.

Paul is going a little further here. He is saying that they are actually better than the letter the Jews of the Old Testament had.[12]

3:7–8

7 But if the ministry of death, written and engraved on stones, was glorious, so that the children of Israel could not look steadily at the face of Moses because of the glory of his countenance, which glory was passing away, 8 how will the ministry of the Spirit not be more glorious?

So the letter that "kills" of verse 6 is the letter Moses brought down from Mount Sinai. Read Exodus 34:29–35, where we find Moses, 1,500 years beforehand, coming down from Mount Sinai for his second time with stones he etched. Paul is actually saying that the letters produced by the Spirit of God on hearts of flesh are superior—far superior—to the letters Moses wrote on stone (look at verses 2 and 3 again).

Then, Paul took that preaching he was doing and told the Corinthians that their mere existence as gospel-centered, Christ-exalting, Father-consulting believers was a flesh-and-blood testament to the work of God in their lives. They were better than an endorsement on the back of a book cover. They were living endorsements of the gospel Paul carried to them.

[12] Yet Jeremiah 17:1 speaks of an etching upon the heart which they did already have. This must also be superior to that. Paul was no dummy when it came to knowing the Old Testament. He must have known that the agent of the law had already etched its letters and that the Holy Spirit could walk through and do much, much more. We already know the law was etched on the hearts of each person (Romans 2:15).

Imagine Paul having the audacity to say, "You are more to be desired than the voice of God immediately transferred to stone!" Why can Paul say such a ridiculous thing? Because even though Paul's voice to them in the Corinthian streets is nothing compared to the voice of God to Moses out of Heaven, Moses' tapping and etching on stone is nothing compared to the hammering power of the Holy Spirit upon the heart.

Christian, where is this powerful, booming voice of Heaven, effectively penned by the third person of the Trinity, forever preserved to the glory of God? He is in you![13]

3:9–11

9 For if the ministry of condemnation had glory, the ministry of righteousness exceeds much more in glory. 10 For even what was made glorious had no glory in this respect, because of the glory that excels. 11 For if what is passing away was glorious, what remains is much more glorious.

He says it again. If we all find that we are sinners through the law that we have broken, and if Moses brought us a very obvious manifestation of that law in the Ten Commandments, and if Moses brought that down from Mount Sinai and had so much glory that he had to wear a veil, and if that glory accompanied a ministry of condemnation, then how much more glory accompanies the ministry brought in you by the Holy Spirit? This great ministry, this ministry of glory, is in us. Remember, now, how this is

---

[13] To what degree did Paul mean this with the positive—the grace of God—in Colossians 1:27?

written to those who are flesh-and-blood representations of Paul.

3:12–18

**Therefore, since we have such hope, we use great bold-
ness of speech—**
Well, you must have a lot of hope, Paul. Let us not forget
that he is not speaking out of some theory. He has already
tipped his hand in the first epistle that some of the first
converts—a majority of them—were Jews. Imagine a Jew
turning away from the glory of the law come down from
Mount Sinai on the face of Moses as he held a ministry of
perfection and condemnation.

**13 unlike Moses, *who* put a veil over his face so that the
children of Israel could not look steadily at the end of
what was passing away.**
Moses couldn't even speak boldly? About what, Paul?
About the glory of God! Don't forget, we have seen
"glory" mentioned in verses 7, 8, 9, 10, and 11. All of the
sudden, we know we are dealing with the real and true
glory of God.

Now it is time for us to discuss what the glory of God
is. Context tells us that the glory of God radiated from
Moses' face and was way too bright. It is brightness,
splendor, grandeur, and brilliance. It is Heavenly and ma-
jestic and magnanimous. It is a display of another world.
It took the voice of God from Heaven to the most note-
worthy man on earth, who would carry the most obvious
standard of the strictest Judge to see that it is a splendid

display from another world. It is a bright display of another world, but it is neither the best nor the brightest display from that world.

What, then, is the glory of God? What is the brightest and grandest and most brilliant and obvious and purest and holiest and greatest display of God from Heaven's shores, from Heaven's throne, from the portals of glory, from the rocks of the diamond-dust beaches, from the jasper walls, from the River of Life?

It is that which has been unveiled in our hearts.

How was it unveiled in our hearts? When gospel truth was etched into them by the Holy Spirit. We read in verses 14 through 16 that as the Israelites of the Old Testament were kept from beholding God's glory in the face of Moses, they are, as of the date of Paul's writing of this letter, still veiled.[14]

So again, how was it unveiled in our hearts? When gospel truth was etched into them by the Holy Spirit. Then what did we see? What is Heaven's greatest reality? What are they talking about the most in Heaven? What is the grandest thing Heaven has to offer? Is it new knees? Is it a new back? Is it pain-free hands or feet? Is it a clear mind? Is it a house on the crystal lake? What does salvation provide first and foremost? The glory of God? Where? In Heaven. Where, primarily? In the main street,

---

[14] The One who etched life and a new director into your hearts is the Lord Himself. Do you need another proof text for the deity of the Holy Spirit? Do you need another proof that the Holy Spirit is God? "Now the Lord is the Spirit" (2 Corinthians 3:17 NKJV)—in this context, the Spirit that wrote upon our hearts.

where the fruit of the tree of life dangles over? In the transparency of the street of gold? Where do I look first in Heaven's domain for the glory to which I have been called, for which I have been saved, because of which I was chosen? Where do I look? I have beheld it in my heart by the Holy Spirit. I look inwardly, and I find rest. I find comfort. I find mercy. I find peace, all by the Holy Spirit, and I am told that within that work is the glory of God— the brightest Heavenly reality. What do I see when I look in my heart that is a mere token of what I will see when I look into Heaven, when my eyelids flicker for the first time in that land of glory?

Answer: The greatest richness of Heaven is found in the face of Jesus Christ (2 Corinthians 4:4–6).

What does this mean? First, that the gospel is a person, not a plan. (Comparing verses 3 and 6 of 2 Corinthians 4, we find that the "gospel is veiled" [NKJV], yet in verse 6 we find that the glory which was veiled is actually the face of Christ.)

Second, that this glory in our hearts is preparing us for the glory in Heaven. See 2 Corinthians 3:18. Why do I feel so out of proportion with what is true in the unseen world? Why do I not feel very glorious today? Answer: You are being changed to fit into that glory once we arrive. See 2 Corinthians 4:7–16.

We cannot quit in our exclamation of the gospel. See 2 Corinthians 4:1–4. Paul would say, "If I have the gospel, in which is found the most amazing treasure of God, a Person named Jesus, and if that Jesus, who is God's greatest treasure, is etched upon the hearts of every believer by the Holy Spirit, then 'every man' (verse 2) among the lost (verse 3) must have eyes opened to the gospel if they will see Heaven or Heaven's treasure, Jesus, or Heaven revealed in themselves through the Holy Spirit. This has much to do with my preaching (verse 5)."

We cannot quit in our adjustment to our perspective. See 2 Corinthians 4:16–18 and the ever-increasing reality that this is just "light affliction … for a moment" (2 Corinthians 4:17 NKJV). In the eons and ages down the hallway of time, this will be a glimmer, a flicker, a blip.

CHAPTER FOUR

Light out of Darkness:
2 Corinthians 4

Look at the connections between 2 Corinthians 4:1–6 and the surrounding passages:

1. Ministry — 4:1 as well as 3:8, 5:18, and 6:3[15]
2. Strong heart — 4:1 as well as 4:16[16]
3. Conscience — 4:2 as well as 1:12 and 5:11
4. Corrupted Word — 4:2 as well as 2:17
5. Perishing and blind ones — 4:3–4 as well as 2:15 and 3:14
6. Gospel — 4:4 as well as 2:12
7. Glory — 4:4 as well as 3:7–11, 3:18, and 4:6, 15, 17

---

[15] Which, of course, is the Greek word for "deacon" and has a number of considerations: 1. This word is more than an "office." 2. The deaconing that is taking place is the "deaconing"/serving up of spirit (3:8), light (3:9), and the gospel (4:4).

[16] In the spirit of Galatians 6:9.

4:1

Therefore, since we have this ministry, as we have received mercy, we do not lose heart.

The tender and compassionate Father—the One we learned about in chapter 1—allows us to find continual strength in a life-giving God and find a cheering influence that does not allow us to lose heart (2 Corinthians 1:8–10). I am amazed at myself, to be honest, that such paltry things take my heart: a single angry member, a single homeowner's issue, a single glitch in my schedule.

4:3–4

3 But even if our gospel is veiled, it is veiled to those who are perishing,

Only those who are lost are blind to the glory. There is no middle group: there are none who are unsaved but seeing. This is why the victory parade is the smell of death to many (2 Corinthians 2:14–16). Let me take it one step further: Those who can see the glory of God in the face of Christ will be saved. There are none who can see but simply won't believe. No, all those who behold the glory of God in the face of Christ will be saved. Otherwise, verse 3 would be incorrect: there would be those who are lost but from whom the gospel is not hidden; they merely ignore it.

4 whose minds the god of this age has blinded, who do not believe, lest the light of the gospel of the glory of Christ, who is the image of God, should shine on them.

May we never underestimate the darkness of the human heart. The problem is not the light. It is the very glory of God, and that glory is not found in the face of Moses (chapter 3) but in the face of Christ (4:6).

The problem is not the message. The gospel is just as plain as it has been ("light of the gospel"). Christ is just as pure as He has been ("who is the image of God"). The problem is not the required response. Anybody can believe, it seems ("who do not believe").

4:5
For we do not preach ourselves, but Christ Jesus the Lord, and ourselves your bondservants for Jesus' sake.

This work of God is primarily through the preached Word of the minister. The minister must also be concerned with the nations.[17,18] Then, notice our share in the labor[19] and the difference we make (4:5).

---

[17] Oddly, those who devalue God's declaration that some will not perish (verse 3) are only those who know there is a reality of people perishing! The very people who have been graced with a knowledge of Christ are often the most critical of the One who graced them when it should make them the more thankful and eager to take this saving work to the world. Perhaps this is you. Might I ask you to spend your energy on spreading grace instead of being angry that you have the grace to begin with?

[18] *God did not make known his ways or reveal his glory or display his marvelous works for you alone, or for your ethnic group alone. He did it with a view to the nations—all the nations, not political states, but nations like the Cherokee Nation, the Navaho Nation, the Waorani Nation. "Peoples" the Psalm calls them;* John Piper, *A Holy Ambition: To Preach Where Christ Has Not Been Named* (Minneapolis, MN: Desiring God, 2011).

[19] In view of my respect for the sovereignty of God, I would never speak of such a responsibility or role if it were not for certain scriptures like 1 Corinthians 3:9, where we are called "labourers together with God" (KJV) or "God's fellow workers" (NKJV).

How do we, mortal people with normal vocabulary, open any person's eyes to see any light in the midst of any darkness? Yet Paul, of all people, knew this when he said at a day in court.

> Acts 26:15-18 So I said, 'Who are You, Lord?' And He said, 'I am Jesus, whom you are persecuting. But rise and stand on your feet; for I have appeared to you for this purpose, to make you a minister and a witness both of the things which you have seen and of the things which I will yet reveal to you. I will deliver you from the Jewish people, as well as from the Gentiles, to whom I now send you, **to open their eyes, in order to turn them from darkness to light, and from the power of Satan to God,** that they may receive forgiveness of sins....

We don't control the blindness, according to 2 Corinthians 4:3–6, but we do control how much we preach. Second Corinthians 4:5 also teaches us that we should never underestimate the power of this same gospel in our own lives: the way in which the gospel drives us to serve others. "Ourselves" is the emphasis in the Greek phraseology (being used in the contrasting phrase, first in the sentence), and Paul is saying that "we don't preach ourselves [only], but rather preach Christ, and [because of that] we preach ourselves as your servants." The Life Application Bible's note says, "Paul willingly served the Corinthians' church even though the people must have deeply disappointed him. Being Christ's follower means serving others, even when they do not measure up to our expectation."[20] That is, a surrendering Savior teaches us to serve others at our expense, to suffer the wrong.[21,22]

We will always feel the choices available to human beings in verse 2, and this is why "Christian moralism" will never, ever work. We are driven by the gospel—not ourselves, but Christ and His gospel—and we are your servants in His stead.

4:6

For it is the God who commanded light to shine out of darkness,

Or, as the ESV states, "For God, who said, 'Let light shine out of darkness,' has shone in our hearts...."

who has shone in our hearts to *give* the light of the knowledge of the glory of God in the face of Jesus Christ.

Never underestimate the necessity of the working of God in the darkened heart. You could pull back 2 Corinthians and see Genesis: Jesus, in verse 4, is the perfect crown of God's creation[23] in the great fulfillment of Genesis

---

[20] Note on 2 Corinthians 4:5 from 1991 publishing.

[21] As 1 Corinthians 6:7 says in answer to the lawsuit question.

[22] Or as the Puritan prayed, "If thy mercy had bounds, where would be my refuge from just wrath?
But thy love in Christ is without measure. Thus, I present myself to thee."Arthur Bennett, ed., *The Valley of Vision, A Collection of Puritan Prayers and Devotions* (Carlisle, PA: Banner of Truth Trust, 2014), 226.

[23] This is the analogy that, sure enough, causes trouble for those of the Arian persuasion who believe that Jesus is created. He is called the "Beginning of the creation of God" (Revelation 3:14 NKJV).
See "Kill the Dragon, Get the Girl"/"Ultimate Exodus" (depending

1:26.[24] So, knowing that the Genesis talk is on the author's mind, consider that he speaks here of the person's heart being lit in the same way that he speaks of the first light being turned on in creation week (Genesis 1:3). If you had nothing to do with creation week, you had nothing to do with your spiritual birthday. Your faith, therefore, must be a gift dispensed through the preaching of the gospel.

4:7–5:1

But we have this treasure in earthen vessels, that the excellence of the power
The ESV says "the surpassing power."

may be of God and not of us.
This and 5:1 form the bookends of this passage. "Earthen vessels" here and "earthly house" (5:1 NKJV) form the thought of Paul, or at least a continuation. "Earthen" refers not to the planet but to the matter out of which our "house" or "tent" was made. The idea that it is called a "tent" refers to the temporary nature, as seen in 4:18. The "glory of God in the face of Jesus" (4:6 NKJV) made clear by the indwelling Holy Spirit (3:2–3) is that which indwells our dirt-made house.

---

on the edition) and commentary on Revelation 3:14 or listen to this: http://www.sermonaudio.com/sermoninfo.asp?SID=12912921181 [accessed 9-26-16].

[24] More can be found by reading the contrasts of Paul in Romans 5 or 1 Corinthians 15. There are some clear references to this in Revelation 5 as well. See commentary in above note or listen here: http://www.sermonaudio.com/sermoninfo.asp?SID=1131365752 [accessed 9-26-16].

An earthen vessel is "quintessentially fragile," prone to breakage, easily chipped and cracked. A breakable vessel offers no protection for the treasure (except from dust and water). The image therefore serves to emphasize the contrast between Paul's own pitiful weakness and the great power of God.[25]

Let us notice some connections to the preceding passage:

1. **"For Jesus' sake"** (4:11 as well as 4:5) — Just as Paul says that he and his companions were serving the people on behalf of Jesus (4:5), so he is delivered to death on behalf or instead of Jesus. Why? Because of the grace needed by the Corinthians. Because of the sins they committed against God, they needed grace to "spread through" them (4:15). Paul served the people because of Christ and His gospel (4:5), resulting in a death Paul would die for Christ (4:11).

2. **"We do not lose heart"** (4:16 as well as 4:1) — Paul tells them this on the heels of the news that we have a superior truth, more even than those who saw Moses after he saw God face to face, and also after revealing to them the reality that he must die for that same wonderful message. In both cases, he uses the phrase "we do not lose heart" as a result of some stunning

---

[25] David E. Garland, *2 Corinthians*, vol. 29, The New American Commentary (Nashville: Broadman & Holman Publishers, 1999), 221.

news. So what is so great about dying the death of Christ? Verses 10 and 11 close with these in almost parallel form.

3.   **"We are earthen vessels" followed by confidence in the God of the gospel** (4:7–14 as well as 1:9–10)

8 *We are* hard-pressed on every side, yet not crushed; *we are* perplexed, but not in despair; 9 persecuted, but not forsaken; struck down, but not destroyed—10 always carrying about in the body the dying of the Lord Jesus...

This, along with "earthen vessels" (NKJV) or "jars of clay" (ESV) in verse 7, gives us the understanding that Paul is saying, "We're just about to break." He follows this talk of feebleness and vulnerability with hope, as we stated, in the gospel. In the first chapter, this gospel is found in verse 10, and he continues to make reference to the gospel in chapter 4, such as in verse 14.

We stated that Paul was dying on behalf of Jesus. When you speak for Jesus and serve for Jesus, you end up dying on His behalf. Jesus cannot die again. He is raised to live "forevermore" (Revelation 1:18 NKJV). So those doing His work in His stead die in His stead. Do not think that we strangers on planet Earth are to be spent for any other worthy cause. It takes no genius to see this same phrase used in verses 10-12 and 16, as well as in 5:1, and to know that dying Christ's death—being defined as that which is brought upon us because we carry Christ's message—is the expectation of the minister of this wonderful new covenant of the Spirit, this covenant of glory found "in the face of Jesus Christ" (2 Corinthians 4:6 NKJV).

15 For all things *are* for your sakes, that grace, having spread through the many, may cause thanksgiving to abound to the glory of God.
That's, once again, his concern.[26] What we find in the face of Christ, we carry in our bodies (4:7) as it was written on our hearts (3:2–3) and we share with others through our service in His name (4:5), and we anticipate gladness pouring out to the Father.

5:1 For we know that if our earthly house, *this* tent, is destroyed, we have a building from God, a house not made with hands, eternal in the heavens.
As opposed to "temporary" on earth (4:18). He seems pretty uninterested in dabbling with temporary and trite things when we are carrying around eternity in our bosoms.

---

[26] Did you notice the absence of preoccupation Paul has with the world? He's not talking about politics, because the believer's country is in his community of faith and his citizenship is in Heaven. His or her energy is to be towards the ones with whom he or she is sojourning, and his or her attention is to be on the payoff for the labor in the Lord.

CHAPTER FIVE

"Ambassadors of Christ": 2 Corinthians 5

5:1

For we know that if our earthly house, this tent, is destroyed, we have a building from God, a house not made with hands, eternal in the heavens.

The idea that the earth is called a "tent" shows the temporary nature as seen in 4:18. The "glory of God in the face of Jesus" (4:6 NKJV) made clear by the indwelling Holy Spirit (3:2–3) is that which indwells our dirt-made house. And this is precisely why Paul says that our readiness for this new house in the skies is from this same Holy Spirit (5:5).

5:2–4

For in this we groan,

This is mentioned again in verse 4. It is like tremors before an earthquake. We are ready to crack and hard to keep together (we are, after all, clay pots [4:7]). There is a sense that things are not exactly as they have been designed. Have you ever felt that way, like things are not the way they ought to be? Every groaning of your soul is a witness that you are not as you have been created and are not as you shall be.

earnestly desiring to be clothed with our habitation
Contextually, this cannot be that which Jesus described as "many mansions" in His "Father's house" (John 14:2 NKJV). This is something that must fit the context. If our earthly, dirt-wrought bodies are the temporary housing, then the heavenly housing is that which we get after the dirt-wrought house is "destroyed" (2 Corinthians 5:1 NKJV).

which is from heaven, 3 if indeed, having been clothed, we shall not be found naked.
Having seen the Genesis 1 reference in 2 Corinthians 4:6 and the Genesis 2 reference in 2 Corinthians 4:16 ("outward man is perishing" [NKJV]), it seems obvious to see the Genesis 3 reference in 2 Corinthians 5:3. In other words, when we arise in the last day, we will be as we were first in the garden: clothed in God's glory, living in God's presence, having access to the tree of life, but totally "not ... found naked" (2 Corinthians 5:3 NKJV). A trip to Genesis 3 would help us discover that they found themselves to be naked after not finding shame in said nakedness first found in Genesis 2. Sin, then, with Eve was so debasing of God's image (remember, 2 Corinthians 4:4 says Christ is now the "image of God" [NKJV]) that there

was no resemblance between the original and the reflection, and they saw themselves as "naked." Well, no more. Because of Christ, we have a day coming when we shall be properly clothed in the glory once had.

4 For we who are in *this* tent groan, being burdened, not because we want to be unclothed, but further clothed, that mortality may be swallowed up by life. This groaning is that witness that says a resurrection awaits the believer, according to 1 Corinthians 15 (particularly 15:51ff).[27]

5:5
Now He who has prepared us for this very thing *is* God, who also has given us the Spirit as a guarantee.

---

[27] I wonder if Paul knew anything about the resurrection's nature at this point. Was 1 Thessalonians written afterward? He seems to have an understanding that "we groan" awaiting the redemption of our bodies (2 Corinthians 5:2; Romans 8:18–24 NKJV) while here he seems to place it not at the resurrection but at death (2 Corinthians 5:1). He also understands that there is "mortality ... swallowed up" (2 Corinthians 5:4 NKJV) when our bodies are changed (1 Corinthians 15:51), but he seems to connect that changing to this body being "destroyed" and our being "clothed with" a "house" that is "eternal in the heavens" (2 Corinthians 5:1–4 NKJV). In other words, I am not sure I see him distinguishing between death and resurrection until he speaks of saints "who are asleep" returning with Christ (1 Thessalonians 4:13–18 NKJV).
We already know that 1 Corinthians 15:24–25 shows almost no distinction between the second coming of Christ and the eternal kingdom (no millennium) and was perhaps somewhat informed by John's Revelation 20:1–6. So is he morphing two events (death and resurrection) into one event in 2 Corinthians 5:1–8 in the same manner?

See notes under verse 1. We'll just add here that the Spirit who has clothed us inwardly in glory is preparing us for glory. This thought is introduced and this point argued since 3:18.

5:6–8
So *we are* always confident, knowing that while we are at home in the body we are absent from the Lord.
Being "in the body" is the emphasis here, and it is in distinction to the "house" that is "eternal in the heavens" (5:1 NKJV).

7 For we walk by faith, not by sight. 8 We are confident, yes, well pleased rather to be absent from the body and to be present with the Lord.
In Philippians 1:23–24, Paul basically says, "You are the only reason I am here."

Furthermore, while there appears to be a gap between having the "earthen vessels" (NKJV) or "jars of clay" (ESV) of 2 Corinthians 4:7 and the heavenly body of 5:1, Paul helps remove ambiguity in this very passage regarding what is typically known as the "intermediate state." He leaves no room for what is commonly referred to as soul sleep.

5:9
Therefore
Since we are away from Christ in this clay-pot body (4:7) and we are being made ready by the Holy Spirit (5:5).

we make it our aim, whether present or absent, to be well pleasing to Him.

It is a good idea to bring Him pleasure. It's nearly impossible to do this accidentally. Nobody just so happens to please God. "Everyone who is mindful of their mortality must therefore be mindful of their morality."[28]

Think about the reality that you can please God. That truly is a wonder.

> Proverbs 11:1 Dishonest scales are an abomination to the LORD, But a just weight is **His delight.**
>
> Proverbs 11:20 Those who are of a perverse heart are an abomination to the LORD, But the blameless in their ways are **His delight**.
>
> Proverbs 12:22 Lying lips are an abomination to the LORD, But those who deal truthfully are **His delight**.
>
> Proverbs 15:8 The sacrifice of the wicked is an abomination to the LORD, But the prayer of the upright is **His delight**.

5:10

For we must all appear before the judgment seat [or "tribunal" (HCSB)[29]] **of Christ,**

---

[28] David E. Garland, *2 Corinthians*, vol. 29, The New American Commentary (Nashville: Broadman & Holman Publishers, 1999), 266.

[29] There is an opinion that only rewards will be given out for believers based on the notion that the *bema* seat has a background found in Greek Olympic-type games where rewards were given out. Consider that this same word is used of Pilate's seat (Matthew 27:19; John 19:13), Herod's seat (Acts 12:21), Gallio's seat (Acts 18:12, 16, 17), Festus's seat (Acts 25:6, 17), and Caesar's seat (Acts 25:10). Were

Since we know that the glory of God is found "in the face of Jesus Christ" (4:6 NKJV), allow me to plead with you to set your heart aright for the glory you shall see, literally, in that face.

that each one may receive the things *done* in the body,
I find this fascinating. He is going back to the body we now have. In the middle of our imagining how things will be, may we not forget about the accountability we have for how things are.

according to what he has done, whether good or bad.
Perhaps most sobering in light of 1:14 and 4:14 is the reality that we are preparing together. This is a personal application that has corporate ramifications that are quite eternal.

5:11–12
Knowing, therefore, the terror of the Lord, we persuade men;
Apparently, our work is vital to the readiness of others.

but we are well known to God, and I also trust are well known in your consciences.
The consciences of his listeners are such a big deal. He mentioned it just a chapter ago and was confident that not only was he clear about how he was conducting himself

---

these guys just interested in *rewarding* Jesus, James, and Paul? Probably not. So, there should be some idea here that more than rewards will be given out at the Judgment Seat of Christ, which will be attended by all believers.

(1:12), but his listeners would likewise be clear about how Paul and his companions conducted themselves (4:2). Here, Paul is not merely satisfied with God knowing them, but rather God and the listeners knowing them clearly.

12 For we do not commend ourselves again to you, but give you opportunity to boast on our behalf, that you may have *an answer* **for those who boast in appearance and not in heart.**
When you need proof of somebody who is living life in the face of those who are simply letting themselves off the hook all the time, point to us. When you meet a dishonest Christian who says, "Only God can judge me," remember there are some of us who have lived before you in a pure conscience and have appealed to—when all is said and done—your consciences.

5:13–14a
For if we are beside ourselves, *it is* **for God; or if we are of sound mind,** *it is* **for you.**
Exactly how crazy does someone get when he has a heart-throbbing desire to keep his daughter pure (11:2)?

14 For the love of Christ
The original allows for Paul's love for Christ or Christ's love for him to be the motive here. In any case, it is the second motivation[30] found for Paul to carry on in his ministry, the ministry he was given beginning in chapter 3 and

---

[30] The "terror of the Lord" (2 Corinthians 5:11 NKJV) being the first.

the ministry for which he would not quit—the "ministry of reconciliation" (5:18–21 NKJV).

compels us,

Or perhaps, in view of 2:14, we are dealing with Christ pulling us along as we are told that this could be a pushing or pulling as context may dictate.[31] Of course, we see how his "craziness" was driven by "the love of Christ." You do some amazingly weird things when you love somebody.

5:14b–15a

because we judge thus: that if One died for all, then all died; 15 and He died for all,

He says it a second time: this *huper* carries the "on behalf of" idea. That is to say, if He did not die, we would have to die. He carried the death of those to whom the death actually belonged.

If you take this along with the entirety of verse 15, you see that "then all died" refers to a time when each and every person *died.*

So when did all die?[32] We must have died when Jesus died. I see the epistles of Paul as a grand harmony much like the Gospels, only they are narrative and these are instruction. Just like the Gospels have similar messages and should only be consulted to give greater light to each

---

[31] David E. Garland, *2 Corinthians*, vol. 29, The New American Commentary (Nashville: Broadman & Holman Publishers, 1999), 277.

[32] We have a choice, of course: 1. *"all died"* in the Garden of Eden; 2. *"all died"* when Christ died; 3. *"all died"* individually as they reached the age of accountability. Why do we pick a team? Verses like Romans 6:6, Galatians 2:19–20, and Colossians 3:3.

other, so these epistles quoted below help us pick the interpretation of what **"then all died"** means. All died in Christ.

> Romans 6:5-11 For if **we have been united together in the likeness of His death**, certainly we also shall be in the likeness of His resurrection, 6 knowing this, that **our old man was crucified** with Him, that the body of sin might be done away with, that we should no longer be slaves of sin. 7 For he who has died has been freed from sin. 8 Now **if we died with Christ**, we believe that we shall also live with Him, 9 knowing that Christ, having been raised from the dead, dies no more. Death no longer has dominion over Him. 10 For the death that He died, He died to sin once for all; but the life that He lives, He lives to God. 11 Likewise you also, **reckon yourselves to be dead indeed to sin**, but alive to God in Christ Jesus our Lord.

> Galatians 2:19-21 For **I through the law died** to the law that I might live to God. 20 **I have been crucified with Christ**; it is no longer I who live, but Christ lives in me; and the life which I now live in the flesh I live by faith in the Son of God, who loved me and gave Himself for me. 21 I do not set aside the grace of God; for if righteousness comes through the law, then Christ died in vain.

> Colossians 3:1-10 If then you were raised with Christ, seek those things which are above, where Christ is, sitting at the right hand of God. 2 Set your mind on things above, not on things on the earth. 3 **For you died**, and your life is hidden with Christ in God. 4 When Christ who is our life appears, then you also will appear with Him in glory. 5 Therefore put to death your members which are on the earth: fornication, uncleanness, passion, evil desire, and covetousness, which is idolatry. 6 Because of these things the wrath of God is coming upon the sons of

disobedience, 7 in which you yourselves once walked when you lived in them. 8 But now you yourselves are to put off all these: anger, wrath, malice, blasphemy, filthy language out of your mouth. 9 Do not lie to one another, since **you have put off the old man with his deeds**, 10 and have put on the new man who is renewed in knowledge according to the image of Him who created him....

If you think about it, this has an amazing rebuttal for those who limit the atonement of Christ to a few. You see, if He did not die for all, then all did not die. One was in the place of all, therefore all must be looked upon as dead; one has made expiation, for the offence of all, therefore all are to be looked upon as having suffered punishment.[33]

5:15b–17
that those who live
So, after learning that "all died" (5:14 NKJV), we find that only a few live. Remember, the context is saying that all died at Calvary, but only some live.

should live no longer for themselves, but for Him who died for them and rose again.
We may ask God, "What do You want from me?" He wants evidence that we've been touched by saving grace. "Men must be brought into a state of grace, before we can expect from them the works of grace."[34]

[33] John Peter Lange et al., *A Commentary on the Holy Scriptures: 2 Corinthians* (Bellingham, WA: Logos Bible Software, 2008), 96.
[34] Richard Baxter and William Orme, *The Practical Works of the Rev. Richard Baxter*, vol. 14 (London: James Duncan, 1830), 121.

16 Therefore, from now on, we regard no one according to the flesh. Even though we have known Christ according to the flesh, yet now we know Him thus no longer. 17 Therefore, if anyone is in Christ,
The tragedy is that with all this talk about an entire world being dead (5:14) and an entire world being turned towards God (5:19), there are only a few, comparatively, who are in the "new creation" (5:17 NKJV) understanding.

he is a new creation;
Here, then, is the fourth reference to the book of Genesis, and this should really seal it for those who have not bought the theme thus far.[35]

Why do we not think the way we used to think? More specifically, why do we not see things the way we used to see them? Because we are new creations. We have a new way of living (5:15b) that is driven—or at least should be—by the new way of thinking (5:16) wrought by the new way of being.

So this "if anyone is in Christ" (5:17 NKJV) is the second way in which he finds a group within the "all" who "died" (5:14 NKJV).[36]

Notice the connection between the status and the state of those who say they are newly created through faith in the gospel. Paul, by God's help, is continually saying, "If you are living, then stop living selfishly." See again that

---

[35] Counting 2 Corinthians 4:4, 4:6, and 5:3.
[36] Counting the reference to "those who live" (2 Corinthians 5:15 NKJV).

there is no preoccupation with the affairs of this life. Consider, as a matter of fact, his attitude in 2 Timothy 2:4.

Think of Paul and Peter and James and John and Jude or even Jesus. Were they pro-sex trafficking? Of course not. Pro-slavery? No way. Pro-tax evasion? No. Pro-gay marriage? No. What you will see, though, is that instead of working through government or enlisting in the Roman army or starting revolutions or running from their world to the outer banks of the empire to get away from the constraints, they were, rather, cleaning up the man in the church who wouldn't teach the younger, the woman in the church who wouldn't allow her husband to lead, the pastor who wouldn't lead his people gently into their next phase. I want a biblical perspective on how proportionally to handle how people conduct themselves as citizens of the kingdom of God more than how they endure, for a short season, citizenship of these godless United States.

5:18
Now all things are of God, who has reconciled us to Himself through Jesus Christ, and has given us the ministry of reconciliation,
This is that ministry that is better than the ministry of Moses and that ministry with its glory found in Christ's face (3:12–4:6). This ministry is better than the ministry of Moses since it is stipulated in hearts by the Spirit instead of "on tablets of stone" to be carried externally (3:2–3 NKJV). So, this Christ-centered, Holy Spirit-driven, God the Father-concocted ministry is for turning the entirety of the world toward Him—and it was done already (see next verse).

5:19–20
that is, that God was in Christ
Here is the second reference to somebody being "in Christ." Here it is the Father. Earlier, it was those who are a "new creation" (5:17 NKJV).

reconciling the world to Himself,
Salvation is God's idea. We're not exactly told the motive in this passage, and so we will not get caught up on the peripheral questions.

not imputing their trespasses to them, and has committed to us the word of reconciliation.
If this is not the prayer of Luke 23:34, what is? Now what if this verse means exactly what it says?

20 Now then, we [Paul and his ambassadors] are ambassadors for Christ, as though God were pleading through us: we implore *you* on Christ's behalf,
For the second time, somebody is acting on somebody's behalf: God in Christ and now Christ in us.
be reconciled to God.
Notice how absent this is of human effort—to include the sinner's prayer or any such mechanism. See, the believer and unbeliever alike are treated as the same in this passage: both were reconciled to God (verse 19) and yet are sought to be reconciled to God (verse 20). This is a second reference to reconciliation as it applies to the sinner who is saved.

5:21

For He made Him who knew no sin *to be* sin for us,

So, a second reference to Christ being a substitute. This time, instead of Jesus dying on behalf of all, He is now being "made ... sin" on behalf of all (5:21 NKJV). We, then, were seen as objects of sin and, therefore, objects of wrath.

that we might become the righteousness of God in Him.

There is a second substitution. He became our sin, and we became His righteousness. This seems rather extreme, doesn't it? Is there any space for a person who thinks he or she is being victimized? Isn't it true that this most extreme measure of sacrificing One's son—making Him the object of your very thoughts of wrath—would far outweigh whatever we are seeing as wrath poured out towards us in this life?

CHAPTER SIX

Unyoking Light from Darkness: 2 Corinthians 6

6:1–2

We then, *as* workers together *with Him* also plead with *you*

Isn't that something? For the second time in this epistle (4:4–6), we have this understanding that it is all God's work being balanced by the reality that we're working with Him.[37] What a tremendous blessing it is to work with God for the reconciliation of others to Himself (given the context carry-over from chapter 5).

> Nothing can wholly satisfy the life of Christ within his followers except the adoption of Christ's purpose toward the world he came to redeem. Fame, pleasure and riches are but husks and ashes in contrast with the boundless and abiding joy of working with God for the fulfillment of his eternal plans. The men who are putting everything

---

[37] He also speaks of it in 1 Corinthians 3:9.

into Christ's undertaking are getting out of life its sweetest and most priceless rewards. (J. Campbell White, "The Layman's Missionary Movement," in *Perspectives on the World Christian Movement: A Reader*, 225)[38]

not to receive the grace of God in vain. 2 For He says:
"In an acceptable time I have heard you,
And in the day of salvation I have helped you."[39]
Behold, now *is* the accepted time; behold, now *is* the day of salvation.
This goes along with verse 1. If you are not going to "be reconciled to God" (5:20 NKJV), then you have received God's grace "in vain" (6:1 NKJV). We are confronted with the question of whether we are dealing with soteriological reconciliation in 5:18 and practical reconciliation in 5:20, but if we do that, then we must also play around with salvation here not being soteriological salvation, which is a paradox at best. How do you have salvation that is not "salvational"?

On the other hand, maybe Paul is using 6:2 to tell us that our practical reconciliation (5:20) is because we have already experienced positional salvation (5:18, 6:2) and that such grace is extended to receive a messenger who seems awkward at times (1 Corinthians 2–4) and authoritarian at others (such as here). If this is not the case, we have a lot of explaining to do for all the times Paul has explained that his conscience is clean (2 Corinthians

---

[38] John Piper, *A Holy Ambition: To Preach Where Christ Has Not Been Named* (Minneapolis, MN: Desiring God, 2011).
[39] Isaiah 49:8.

1:12–14, 4:1–3, 5:10–12), and that is without the very next verse.

If any of this is true, then we must see that Paul is using the quotation to speak of a regular, expected salvation that is ongoing. We are being saved from our sin, and it is being continually reconciled with our Father (5:20).

6:3

We give no offense in anything, that our ministry may not be blamed.

For the second time since 5:11, we have an appeal to this church by Paul that if he did not lead a blameless life, they probably would care nothing about the gospel. Now, we would probably all admit that Paul was a sinner like you and I, but exactly how sure do we need to be to know that we are living a life void of offense from the perspective of the God we represent and the Son whose name we carry?

Again, what ministry are we talking about? The ministry of reconciliation (5:19–20), the ministry of the Spirit (3:7–8), the ministry of the gospel of Jesus (4:6). We must take personal responsibility for how the teaching of Christ is perceived by the world. Yes, the teaching of Christ.

Look to what extent Paul went to preserve that "clean as a whistle" reputation for Christ's sake among the collective conscience of these followers of Christ:

6:4–11

11 O Corinthians! We have spoken openly to you, our heart is wide open.

How do we prove that we have "big hearts" for you in the gospel (reaching back to the preceding chapter) if we haven't convinced you yet (with verses 4–10)? Consider 11:22–33.

6:12–17
You are not restricted by us, but you are restricted by your *own* affections.
Between hesitating affections towards Paul and his companions (as can be seen in the appeal to the grace they've received from them to begin with [5:13–21]) and the misdirected affections towards ungodly objects of affections in the following verses (6:14–17), they were restricted in their love.

By the way, it seems a little odd that God's ambassadors would be hesitatingly received. Paul is saying, "Here we are asking you to be reconciled to God and acknowledge your place in this grand plan for your redemption, and we still feel like we are unloved as God's messengers." This does not go away. We see in 2 Corinthians 12:15 that he feels so very troubled. His credentials are the sufferings he has endured from the enemy, and he feels as though he should (as he did in chapters 1 and 2 and as he alludes to in the next chapter) receive some reciprocation.

Do we see that the unwillingness to cut ourselves from worldly alliances in favor of God's message and His messengers is because we love idols (6:14–17)? Imagine just how much this would affect us if we exercised it? Do you see that pseudo-apostles (11:13–15) are what we're talking about? If that was the original context and if these false apostles are in their church, how could it be any less intense of an application with false Christians who seep into the church? That gives a fundamental obligation upon the believer not only to be examining him- or herself (13:5), but to know that others are to be likewise examining themselves (13:6).

It is such an unfortunate thing when those in the church will not see those who are pulling them down in their reputations and in their character.

CHAPTER SEVEN

"Comforted in Your Comfort": 2 Corinthians 7

7:1

Therefore, having these promises, beloved,
This must be a reference to the two closing verses of the previous chapter. Since we have the promise of God being a Father to us, having one promise (6:17) and then another (6:18) leads the reader to remember that there is at least some license to see the Old Testament as a book of promises.

let us cleanse ourselves from all filthiness of the flesh and spirit, perfecting holiness
This goes in concert with the talk about connections, commitments, and alliances in 6:14–16 and the need to separate in 6:17.

in the fear of God.

Remember that in the context of all of this, Paul is saying, "Validate us and not them" (1 Corinthians 9:1–7; 2 Corinthians 11:1–15). In the context of this passage, we get the understanding that holiness is something that involves turning from false teachers or intrusive apostles. If that's not it, why open (6:13) and close (7:2) with an appeal to honor his office? We are to be excellent separators, "perfecting holiness" (7:1 NKJV). "The verb 'to perfect' *(epitelein)* means 'to bring to completion,' 'to bring to its intended goal'."[40] This is not easy, and it takes intention. "Perfecting holiness" takes moments of deciding against pleasing yourself, oftentimes chemically since moments of sin typically release baths of euphoric chemistry into our brains.

Remember, the appeal of 6:12 is that they "are restricted by [their] own affections." Contextually, people cannot separate from false teachers or divisive people when they decide they love them more than they should actually love them.

Also, we see that God is a Father to us in a wonderful way as we take on the spirit of this passage (6:18). We know that the passage requires separation from intrusive and divisive teachers, but this carries the idea of the Spirit of God saying to His children, "Just play the part of the son, and I will play the part of the dad."

The reason we find this hard to embrace is because it can sound like salvation by works or "stop sinning to

---

[40] David E. Garland, *2 Corinthians*, vol. 29, The New American Commentary (Nashville: Broadman & Holman Publishers, 1999), 342.

clean yourself up," but we are not talking about earning salvation. We are talking about being energized by salvation. Christ did this for us (5:14–15), and we find reason and energy to do for Him.

Our view of salvation often complicates this. We say things like, "You can be no more right with God than you are in Christ." That's true as far as our position, but here Paul speaks to people who are God's kids and yet offers them the opportunity—or, rather, commands them—to live the part of God's kids. So, there really is a reality of pleasing the Father more.

Come on, though, how does one separate unto holiness? How does one decide from whom he or she should separate? Can you totally leave the world? We've already seen that the context speaks specifically of false teachers and, by extension, counterfeiting Christians.

Paul was kind enough to help us a little further: We separate from the pseudo-Christian (1 Corinthians 5:10–11) and from misuse of a culture of death known as "the world." We are to be using the system (1 Corinthians 7:29–31) while still creating emotional distance, living as independently as possible, and supporting the body of Christ as much as possible.

7:2

Open *your hearts* to us.
This is a rehearsal, almost a chorus, from 6:13. Both 6:13 and 7:2 are responses to the open heart of Paul (6:11). This is the answer to the misdirected affections earlier in the passage.

We have wronged no one, we have corrupted no one, we have cheated no one.
This really is the conclusion to the passage from Paul. He is saying, "Look, let's cleanse ourselves from the filthiness of misdirected affections and closed hearts to each other." Are you awaiting somebody to take steps toward maturity before you do? Maybe we should be the grown-ups in the conversation. "This is the hardest and the happiest business in the world."[41]

7:4–7

4...I am filled with comfort. ... 7 and not only by his coming, but also by the consolation with which he was comforted in you, when he told us of your earnest desire, your mourning, your zeal for me, so that I rejoiced even more.
Here we see the power of encouragement. Please see that the Corinthian church's desire to be a forgiving church was a particular encouragement to the apostle. Have you considered that this is why some choose not to forgive? Have you seen that the reason we don't forgive is because it causes the other party to carry a heavy, heavy weight within him or her?

7:8–11

8 For even if I made you sorry with my letter, I do not regret it; though I did regret it. For I perceive that the same epistle made you sorry, though only for a while.

---

[41] John Piper, *A Holy Ambition: To Preach Where Christ Has Not Been Named* (Minneapolis, MN: Desiring God, 2011).

9 Now I rejoice, not that you were made sorry, but that your sorrow led to repentance.

It is interesting to note that sorrow and repentance are not the same. May pastors be quick to remember a good warning on self-preach from Mr. Baxter:

> The sorrow of Repentance may be without the change of heart and life; because a passion may be easier wrought than a true Conversion; but the change cannot go without some good measure of the sorrow. Indeed, we may justly here begin our confessions: it is too common with us to expect that from our people, which we do little or nothing in ourselves. What pains take we to humble them, while ourselves are unhumbled! How hard do we press them by all our expostulations, convictions, and aggravations, to wring out of them a few penitent tears, (and all too little) when our own eyes are dry, and our hearts are little affected with remorse, and we give them an example of hardheartedness, while we are endeavouring by our words to mollify and melt them.[42]

For you were made sorry in a godly manner, that you might suffer loss from us in nothing. 10 For godly sorrow produces repentance *leading* to salvation,

Again, when we see the switching back and forth between salvation wrought by God at Calvary (5:18) and salvation wrought by God and the preacher at the moment of faith, to be experienced thereafter in the life of the Christian (5:20–6:2), one has to wonder if he is referencing salvation as something they should fear losing. I hesitate to answer on the grounds that it may cost me readers, but in

---

[42] Richard Baxter and William Orme, *The Practical Works of the Rev. Richard Baxter*, vol. 14 (London: James Duncan, 1830), 133.

view of 2 Corinthians 11:1–15, does it not appear that if they leave Paul, they leave his message? Is not his message the gospel? Is not the gospel the message that saves when one continues to believe in it (1 Corinthians 15:1–2)? Is not this context one of following Paul's leadership in the application of forgiveness?

The most frightening thing, then, is that these folks wanted to exercise church discipline because of the gospel (1 Corinthians 5:7 compared with 2 Corinthians 2:7 does lead us to believe that they did, in fact, separate from this man) and then withhold forgiveness by some other standard.

> We would think that those who were Christians would already have the assurance of salvation.[102438] But Paul's worries about the Corinthians (see 5:20; 6:1, 14–7:1) are evident. Later in the letter, he will express his fear that not all will have repented of the "impurity, sexual sin and debauchery in which they have indulged" (12:21).[44]

7:11–12

11 For observe this very thing, that you sorrowed in a godly manner: What diligence it produced in you, *what clearing of yourselves, what* indignation, *what* fear, *what* vehement desire, *what* zeal, *what* vindication! In

---

[431028] *T. Gad* 5:7 is apropos: "For according to God's truth, repentance destroys disobedience, puts darkness to flight, illumines the vision, furnishes knowledge of the soul, and guides the deliberative power to salvation."

[44] David E. Garland, *2 Corinthians*, vol. 29, The New American Commentary (Nashville: Broadman & Holman Publishers, 1999), 356.

all *things* you proved yourselves to be clear in this matter.

Have you noticed what a clean conscience can do? Have you noticed that when you feel lighter through repentance and reconciliation, you take a vengeance on your "old self"? That is the result of "godly sorrow": "repentance" (7:10 NKJV). Repentance is described in verse 11 as standing on God's team against yourself. If you repent of strange ideologies and anti-holiness that creep up and you speak against them (10:4–5), you stand on God's team against the mediocre standards of so-called "good."

> When a man is conformed to the mind of God, or is troubled by a regard to God on account of his sins, he will turn from those sins with all his heart; and he will become totally opposed to all that once was pleasant or seemed indifferent to him (μετάνοια).[45]

The power of a moving, clean conscience will make you do things that the fear of the Lord (5:11) and the love of Christ (5:14) prod you to do. Behold, the power of a clean conscience. What have you stood against recently? If nothing, you've repented of nothing. You've changed your mind about nothing.

One more thing, church: this was a collective thing. Paul is talking to a church. They took action. Churches take collective action through voting membership. How else would Titus have had reason to tell Paul that the

---

[45] John Peter Lange et al., *A Commentary on the Holy Scriptures: 2 Corinthians* (Bellingham, WA: Logos Bible Software, 2008), 129.

church had taken action? We can't simply say that the elders did it on behalf of the people like a democratic republic, for how would they have enforced their non-voting or non-present members at the individual level? If it were not the choice of the individual, this would have been an obligatory, authoritarian chore indeed.

12 Therefore, although I wrote to you, *I did* not *do it* for the sake of him who had done the wrong, nor for the sake of him who suffered wrong, but that our care for you in the sight of God might appear to you.
Here we see the gravity of dissension. Imagine sending somebody such a distance away. Titus went 250 miles away—500 miles away from where Paul intended to minister (Troas; 2:12). It was important enough to be separated in that ancient world from a dear friend to make sure there was no division in the body that was outside of the scope of gospel-esque forgiveness. This is the value of one believer.

***I did* not *do it* for the sake of him who had done the wrong,**
However, this is more to show us the value of the church.

nor for the sake of him who suffered wrong, but that our care for you
Great effort and mental energy were expended on this clarity in the church. A man like me wonders how many pastors would be bored if they were concerned with helping their churches perfect (1) accountability, as in 1 Corinthians, and (2) forgiveness, as in here.

7:13–16

Therefore we have been comforted in your comfort. And we rejoiced exceedingly more for the joy of Titus, because his spirit has been refreshed by you all. ... 15 And his affections are greater for you as he remembers the obedience of you all, how with fear and trembling you received him.

Can we just remind ourselves that this was Titus preaching the message of the apostles? Can we just remind ourselves that the church shared in the "Apostles' Doctrine"? I will furthermore remind us that when somebody preaches the words of the apostles as Titus did here, it emphasizes not only the strategy of preaching but, and we say this carefully, the timeliness of preaching—that the message of the apostles is both planned and momentarily necessary. Imagine the effectiveness of one man who brings the message to a people, doing the will of God, allowing himself to be carried by the will of God, and finding refreshment from the people of God as in verse 13.

CHAPTER EIGHT

Sowing Bountifully:
2 Corinthians 8–9

8:1–4
1 Moreover, brethren,
Since "I have confidence in you in everything" (7:16 NKJV)…

we make known to you the grace of God bestowed on the churches of Macedonia:

1. This takes place at the same time as the events of Acts 20; we're just not told about it.
2. This chapter refers back to the journey from Troas to Macedonia, looking for Titus (2 Corinthians 2:12–13.
3. While Paul and Timothy were in Macedonia awaiting Titus (concerned about the Corinthian church's reaction to his third letter, which we do

not have), they spent time around Macedonian believers (8:1–4).

4. Paul already mentioned (1 Corinthians 16) that on one of his journeys through Macedonia he would like to collect an offering for the saints in Jerusalem.

5. Just as Titus carried the third letter (which we do not have), Titus would carry this fourth letter (which we call "Second Corinthians"). See 2 Corinthians 8:6, 16–18.

This was simple benevolence giving. One can see that this was an opportunity-driven offering (gift) and, as both 8:10 and 9:2 point out, begun a year ago. This gives us the relative amount of time elapsed since the writing of 1 Corinthians, particularly chapter 16:1–6: one year. One might even notice the talk of "Macedonia" in that passage as well as this one (2 Corinthians 7:5). So this trip about which we read may have been considered an opportunity that was supposed to happen second-hand instead of an actual trip from Paul. Consider 2 Corinthians 8:13–14 as more information is given about this instance:

> 2 Corinthians 8:13-14 For I do not mean that others should be eased and you burdened; 14 but by an equality, that now at this time your abundance may supply their lack, that their abundance also may supply your lack— that there may be equality.

This was not "class welfare" but rather corporate care. This was an instance-driven love offering. This was not meant to be a protracted arrangement over years and even generations of time, where a church did nothing, moved nowhere, and in decades still expected offerings from Corinth through the apostle.

8:8–9
8 I speak not by commandment,
This is not compulsory.

but I am testing the sincerity of your love
Contextually, the reader is drawn back to 5:14 and the lasting influence of gospel love.

by the diligence of others. 9 For you know the grace of our Lord Jesus Christ, that though He was rich, yet for your sakes He became poor, that you through His poverty might become rich.
Once again, Paul appeals to the gospel[46] to drive home his request. Paul knows that his greatest joy is to see gospel-reflective, abundant sacrifice in the lives of the believers (9:6), which will produce fruit that coincides with that of the Christ who gave of His life in that very same gospel (9:11–14). The gospel preaching was that which made particular people credentialed in the lives of fellow churches (8:18). This is not something that occurs once in the life of the believer.

---

[46]Just as he did in the previous chapter for the restoration of the disciplined brother.

8:11–12

We have two things happening here. First, Paul doesn't care what your motive was a year ago. If you made a commitment, follow through ("complete the doing of it" [8:11 NKJV]). Secondly, this is supposed to be, after all is said and done, a rational decision ("willing mind" [8:12 NKJV]).

8:19–21

and not only *that,* but who was also chosen by the churches

Is that a fact? Another proof text of congregational action? This was not a democratic republic where the elders chose. No, we had the precedence of individuals within the congregation giving a collective forgiveness to an offender (see notes on 7:11).

to travel with us with this gift,

Talk about a tremendous spiritual gift in light of 1 Corinthians 12–14.

which is administered by us to the glory of the Lord Himself and *to show* your ready mind,

It seems like this means the safeguarding and distribution of the offerings were performed in part by Titus because the churches said so.

20 avoiding this: that anyone should blame us in this lavish gift which is administered by us—21 providing honorable things, not only in the sight of the Lord, but also in the sight of men.

It's probably not possible to be dogmatic here, but it seems that Paul is going out of his way to say that they are including many witnesses in the form of Titus and the man who accompanied him (8:18–19) along with Timothy, to be sure that there is financial transparency and integrity. They would not have minded you seeing an elaborate budget if this were a church business meeting.

8:22–23
22 And we have sent with them our brother whom we have often proved diligent in many things,
The best commentary I can add here is somebody else's:

> The person referred to has been variously identified with Titus' brother, Barnabas, Mark, Luke, and Epaenetus, mentioned in Rom. 16:5. The reference to Epaenetus has been urged on the ground of a supposed play upon the word *praise, epainos;* Epaenetus meaning *praiseworthy....*[47]

but now much more diligent, because of the great confidence which we have in you. 23 If anyone inquires about Titus, he is my partner and fellow worker concerning you. Or if our brethren are inquired about, they are messengers of the churches,
See note on 8:19. Incidentally, Titus and his fellow traveler were the advanced party, so to speak, to keep the Corinthian church from being embarrassed when Paul showed up to receive their offering (9:3–5).

---

[47] Marvin Richardson Vincent, *Word Studies in the New Testament*, vol. 3 (New York: Charles Scribner's Sons, 1887), 332.

the glory of Christ.

messengers of the churches
See this rendering: "Whether as regards Titus, [he is] my companion and fellow-labourer in your behalf; or our brethren, [they are] deputed messengers of assemblies, Christ's glory" (1890 Darby Bible).[48] Perhaps this is a proof text for missionaries going on deputation as many independent churches exercise. When they go and do work among other peoples, they should be deputies of many churches. Perhaps this is an application by extension, but certainly we are not dealing with evangelistic work.

8:24–9:1
9:1 Now concerning the ministering to the saints, it is superfluous for me to write to you;
In other words, "There's precious little more that I should need to say about this...."

9:15
Thanks *be* to God for His indescribable gift!
So let's talk a minute about the gift of giving. Contextually, the reason it is an "indescribable gift" to give is because it is a foretaste of gospel glory to be experienced after this life: the joy of abandoned generosity and sacrifice and the joy of knowing you are really a part of a

---

[48] John Nelson Darby, *The Holy Scriptures: A New Translation from the Original Languages* (Oak Harbor: Logos Research Systems, 1996), 2 Corinthians 8:23.

family—which would mean nothing if we didn't know that's what we started as in the Garden.

CHAPTER NINE

"Mighty in God": 2 Corinthians 10

When we read through a passage of Scripture and see something that is a big deal to the author, we ought to stop and make a big deal of it—particularly as the people of God need the message of God as it was first given. Maybe we should start by reminding ourselves of what Paul says the gospel does (1 Corinthians 15:1–10).

1. The gospel causes us to give (2 Corinthians 9:13).
2. The gospel causes us to go (2 Corinthians 10:14–16).
3. The gospel causes us to guard and grapple against counterfeits (2 Corinthians 11:1–5).
    a. Paul actually believes this is a spiritual altercation (2 Corinthians 10:4–5).
    b. There is a future (this makes a lot of sense in relation to 2 Corinthians 5:10–11 and

5:20). Have you noticed—whether in 2 Corinthians 1:12–14 or here—that Paul is preoccupied with looking at things from the perspective of the future?

4. The gospel causes us to go without a lot.
   a. Paul went without resources (2 Corinthians 11:7–8).
   b. Paul went without both safety and health (2 Corinthians 11:23–28).

10:2–5

2 But I beg you that when I am present I may not be bold with that confidence by which I intend to be bold against some, who think of us as if we walked according to the flesh.

Paul is saying, "I would prefer to stay as gentle as I usually am when I am with you instead of becoming bold—almost brash—as I am in these letters."

3 For though we walk in the flesh, we do not war according to the flesh. 4 For the weapons of our warfare *are* not carnal but mighty in God for pulling down strongholds,

Paul is both defending his uniqueness as Christ's apostle[49] and implying that the enemies (the "some" of verse 2) who

---

[49] He basically restates it in verses 7–11, with verse 7 restating verses 2–3, verse 8 restating verse 4, and verses 9–11 not only contending for his approach but also warning them that they could get the "other Paul approach" if things don't change prior to his arrival. He almost appears to be saying, "I already told you we don't want to

are in and among the Corinthian church—and later identified as "false apostles" (11:13–15 NKJV)—are actually
spiritual enemies of God. *The gospel draws demonic re-
sistance in the form of people.* Paul contends that he
doesn't need to bring carnality to this fight, but rather
weapons which are mighty for the task of dealing with
these imposters (10:4 NKJV).

5 casting down arguments and every high thing [high-
sounding opinion] **that exalts itself against the
knowledge of God, bringing every thought into captivity to the obedience of Christ,**
Paul is furthermore saying that these so-called "arguments" brought on by the "some" of verse 2 are against
the real Christ. Now, this is not a surprise since the next
chapter talks to us about the Christ of the "false apostles"
(11:3–4, 13–15 NKJV). Now, how can these "some" (10:2
NKJV) be so formidable that they require weapons which
are "mighty in God" (10:4 NKJV) and they actually argue
against submission to the real Christ? It must be empow-
ered by a spiritual power. Second Corinthians 11:4 says it
is a "different spirit" that empowers the false apostle to
preach his or her "different gospel" of "another Jesus"
(NKJV).[50]

---

get crazy when we are with you (verse 2), but we'll bring our bold-
ness that expresses itself in our letters the next time we see you if we
have to do so."

[50] I find Strategic Level Spiritual Warfare at first very repugnant. I
have seen this idea of spiritual involvement heavily abused and
have, therefore, resisted it, having deemed it virtually laughable.
However, when I consider references such as Ezekiel 28:10–12 and
Daniel 10:13, I must admit that there is something to these ideas of
national or regional hierarchy.

One must view how the contextual flow of 6:14–7:1 plays in here. We are to be "perfecting holiness in the fear of God" (7:1 NKJV), and we know that only the Holy Spirit can make this happen in the life of the believer (a main point of chapter 3). Here we see that "bringing every thought into captivity" (10:5 NKJV) is a major part of Holy Spirit living after all.[51]

10:6
and being ready to punish all disobedience when your obedience is fulfilled.
Again, Paul promises that he will bring judgment down on these "some" (10:2 NKJV) after the whole of the Corinthian church smashes these contrary opinions of Christ and His gospel which Paul preached. Paul's response on the enemy no doubt dwarfs that "clearing" response of 7:11 (NKJV) performed by the church herself. This is the kind of urgency and accountability that are wrapped up in Paul's gospel-centered approach to life.

10:12–13
12 For we dare not class ourselves or compare ourselves with those who commend themselves.
The gospel draws misplaced measurements of maturity. In other words, when the gospel is too simple (11:3), we must find other ways to measure our worth, to measure our contribution to God, to measure our maturity.

---

[51] See appendix on Spiritual Formation.

But they, measuring themselves by themselves, and comparing themselves among themselves, are not wise. 13 We, however, will not boast beyond measure, but within the limits of the sphere which God appointed us—a sphere which especially includes you.

Here is the tragedy of misplaced measuring sticks. We are not to be measuring ourselves with others who work in our world, but we are to measure ourselves against what we are supposed to be doing with what God has given us, or "appointed us" (10:13 NKJV). In this case, these false apostles and misleading teachers compared themselves not with the message delivered by Christ through His apostles but by other standards within their own group. Maybe it was because they could do miracles (11:13–15) that they did not consider their message, but it seems that this is so contextually. They looked at results amongst each other instead of the meat of their message and the condition of their hearts.

10:14–18

14 For we are not overextending ourselves (as though *our authority* did not extend to you), for it was to you that we came with the gospel of Christ;

This rings quite true with 1 Corinthians 4:10, except now he is not contending for attention among fellow gospel preachers; now he is contending against those who preach a false gospel (2 Corinthians 11:1–4).

15 not boasting of things beyond measure, *that is,* in other men's labors, but having hope, *that* as your faith is increased, we shall be greatly enlarged by you in our

sphere, 16 to preach the gospel in the *regions* beyond you, *and* not to boast in another man's sphere of accomplishment.

Having now mentioned the gospel twice in two verses, it seems that this has much to do with Paul's argument. He is saying, "I got to you and beyond you with the true gospel. It seems like I've earned the right to be heard by you first and foremost." By the way, he's going even beyond that: he speaks of using their maturity—their mature handling of resources—to reach more people once they finally grow up a little. A church has levels of maturity and can handle things only as the members, by and large, grasp certain truths.

> The NIV[52] translation suggests that Paul wants his work to expand among them. But he states in 10:16 that his goal is to preach the gospel in the regions beyond you. In Rom 15:24 we learn that he intends to go to Rome and then on to Spain. Clearly, he wants to settle the problems with the Corinthians so that he can concentrate on missionary endeavors elsewhere with their support. If Paul constantly has to be putting out fires, he cannot move on to new work. But he expresses confidence that the Corinthians' faith will indeed grow. This will allow his area of activity to expand, not in Corinth, but in territory beyond them.[53]

17 But "he who glories, let him glory in the LORD."

---

[52]

[53] David E. Garland, *2 Corinthians*, vol. 29, The New American Commentary (Nashville: Broadman & Holman Publishers, 1999), 456–457.

Here again is a repeat of his letter from one year ago (or less; 1 Corinthians 1:31).

CHAPTER TEN

Workers of Deceit:
2 Corinthians 11

11:5–9

5 For I consider that I am not at all inferior to the most eminent apostles. 6 Even though *I am* untrained in speech, yet *I am* not in knowledge. But we have been thoroughly manifested among you in all things.

Here Paul admits that his expertise is in knowledge rather than rhetoric. He isn't saying he is not a good speaker, but rather that his concentration isn't in professional oratory but in proclamation of truth.[54]

7 Did I commit sin in humbling myself that you might be exalted, because I preached the gospel of God to you free of charge?

---

[54] _____, *NIV Archaeological Study Bible* (Grand Rapids: Zondervan, 2005), 1897.

A professional rhetorical speaker would exact a fee from his listeners for the "knowledge" he imparted.[55]

It should be apparent to the reader that the "gospel of God" being preached is a big deal, having seen it as a major part of his argument in 10:14–15—three times in eleven verses.

11:16–21

16 I say again, let no one think me a fool. If otherwise, at least receive me as a fool, that I also may boast a little.

In other words, "If I am a fool, then at least give me the privilege of a fool."

18 Seeing that many boast according to the flesh, I also will boast. 19 For you put up with fools gladly, since you *yourselves* are wise!

This is pretty sarcastic. If anything is clear to this point, it is that Paul thinks the Corinthian believers are unwise.

20 For you put up with it if one brings you into bondage, if one devours *you,* if one takes *from you,* if one exalts himself, if one strikes you on the face. 21 To *our* shame I say that we were too weak for that!

Again, this is sarcasm. Paul is telling the Corinthians that they are being victimized (slapped), but he is saying, "I guess I'm too soft for that. I can't put up with it." Of course, the irony is that weak people do not endure what Paul lists soon.

---

[55] Ibid.

11:23–28

His third list of suffering in this book (chapters 4 and 7 preceding this).

11:31–33

The God and Father of our Lord Jesus Christ, who is blessed forever, knows that I am not lying. 32 In Damascus the governor, under Aretas the king, was guarding the city of the Damascenes with a garrison, desiring to arrest me; 33 but I was let down in a basket through a window in the wall, and escaped from his hands.

A person must wonder why Paul is referencing this harrowing episode. He's had others since Acts 9! Ephesus (Acts 19) for starters, and then we could mention being whipped and jailed in Philippi (Acts 16). We could talk about Lystra (being stoned doesn't happen all the time; Acts 14). With all of the adventures he mentions in 2 Corinthians 11:24–30, a person would marvel that he names an episode in Acts to begin with. For him then to skip all these in his recollection to speak of one just after his conversion[56] leads one to ask, "Why?" Other commentators are equally as confused: "Why Paul does not continue at this point to pursue this discussion can only be speculated."[57]

---

[56] Really, three years after his conversion; John B. Polhill, *Acts*, vol. 26, The New American Commentary (Nashville: Broadman & Holman Publishers, 1992), 241. He references Galatians 1:17–18.

[57] Jerry Falwell, ed. *Liberty Commentary on the New Testament* (Lynchburg: Liberty Press: 1978), 460.

There are even those who think it was added later based on its strange inclusion: "As we noted, there are those who see these verses as a gloss that has crept into the text."[58]

Anyway, this is the third time this occurs in Scripture—after the spies to Jericho and David.[59]

After it's all been thought through, we reminisce about Jesus' instruction to His disciples about fleeing from one city to the next (Matthew 10:23) and have to admit that there are times when running is best. Even Jesus demonstrated this.[60] Perhaps Chrysostom said it best: "At times when evils were inevitable, grace alone sufficed, but where there were choices to be made, he did not hesitate to seize the opportunity."[61]

In other words, today's believer may feel like it is always time to stand and fight.

It really seems as though Paul is saying, "My credential is continuous suffering. I have been doing it since I was saved." A look at Acts 9 will show us that you don't have to be saved long to: 1. influence those in your area of expertise (synagogue); 2. share your faith (he preached); 3. suffer for Jesus.

---

[58] Ralph P. Martin, *2 Corinthians*, ed. Ralph P. Martin, Lynn Allan Losie, and Peter H. Davids, Second Edition, vol. 40, Word Biblical Commentary (Grand Rapids, MI: Zondervan, 2014), 573.

[59] Marvin Richardson Vincent, *Word Studies in the New Testament*, vol. 3 (New York: Charles Scribner's Sons, 1887), 353.

[60] http://www.sermonaudio.com/sermoninfo.asp?SID=72314195493 [accessed 12/26/16].

[61] Gerald Bray ed., *Ancient Christian Commentary on Scripture, New Testament VII, 1–2 Corinthians* (Downers Grove: Intervarsity: 1999), 301.

CHAPTER ELEVEN

Living by the Power of God: 2 Corinthians 12–13

Let me first give you some clear connections between chapters 11 and 12 to show us that these man-made divisions have weaknesses:

1. The topic of boasting before and after the chapter break and its implication (11:17–18, 11:30, 12:1, 12:5, 12:9, 12:11). Paul wants you to know what he's about versus what his opposition is about

2. The repeat of 11:30 and 12:5 as repetition within an argument

3. The topic of being perceived as a "fool" (11:16–19, 12:6, 12:11). If Paul is going to be thought of as a fool, he wants to decide in what way he will be deemed "foolish."

12:1
It is doubtless not profitable for me to boast. I will come to visions and revelations of the Lord:
Paul is saying, "Now that I have spoken about my credentials as a teacher and preacher (chapter 10) and a sufferer (latter part of chapter 11), I will now discuss my credentials as a man who has heard from the other world."

12:2–9
2 I know a man in Christ who fourteen years ago— whether in the body I do not know, or whether out of the body I do not know, God knows—such a one was caught up to the third heaven.
It seems reasonable to use the Genesis backdrop Paul has already used four times to suggest here that just as there was a third Heaven in Genesis,[62] which would have been high enough for the stars, we are dealing with the throne of God, which is "above the stars" (Isaiah 14:12–14 NKJV).

7 And lest I should be exalted above measure
The inclusion of "this guy Paul knew" is odd enough since he is talking about his own credentials by which he can boast as a true apostle of Christ, but now this inclusion of "lest I should be exalted," speaking of his desire not to be

---

[62] There is a heaven that separates the waters (which may now be missing if the pre-flood canopy theory is legitimate) on the second day. There is a "heavens" that is high enough for the heavenly bodies of the fourth day, and there is a "heavens" low enough that the birds were able to fly in it on the fifth day.

unduly lifted up because of this testimony, should seal it for anybody wondering if Paul is talking about himself.

by the abundance of the revelations, a thorn in the flesh was given to me, a messenger of Satan to buffet me,
An "angel of Satan" has been sent to hurt Paul. Have you ever felt pained and crushed by Satan? Either Paul is horribly preoccupied with Satan (chapter 2 in relation to unforgiveness, chapter 11 in relation to false prophets) or Satan really does hate him. If this is not a literal "angel," then it is at least "Satan through malady."[63] It could be his eyes,[64] and it could be from the time he was stoned (11:25).

lest I be exalted above measure. 8 Concerning this thing I pleaded with the Lord three times that it might depart from me. 9 And
What a tremendous blessing: *"And"* means there is more to the story than "I called, and that's that." *God does indeed hear my prayers.* Have you considered all that He hears and yet He hears your prayer? Isaiah 59:1–2 speaks of His ear being able to hear. There is not a cry He does not hear.

---

[63] This sounds an awful lot like Job.

[64] He expressed to the Galatians in his epistle to them that he wrote them a "large letter" (6:11), which could refer to the size of his print, after writing how sure he was that they would have given him their own eyes (4:15).

At the level of the soil where the feet of earth dwellers trod

He hears the plants break through their sod

—the straining of the grass and the buzzing of the bees

—he hears them all, yet He hears me.

At the level of the leaves,

You hear the wind in the trees,

Staring off to the seas,

He hears them all, and He hears me.

At the clouds as people gawk

He hears the squawking of the hawks

If you think your Friends on Facebook stalk

God hears them all, and He hears me.

Then there's where airplanes fly

Can You hear the noise in the sky?

Solar flares & winds—radiation's cry?

Yes, You hear them all, yet You hear me.

12:9–10

He said to me, "My grace is sufficient for you, for My strength is made perfect in weakness."

It is hard to imagine, but many of you are fully aware that your God and mine visits us in the cold, dark night. He speaks to us when we ask, and here we find the reality that Paul heard the voice of God so clearly that it changed his prayer life. This is informative on so many fronts: God does, in His paternal way, hear every prayer.[65]

He said to me, "My grace is sufficient for you, for My strength is made perfect in weakness."
This is a marvelous truth that our Great God is not weak to the feeble cries of His young. Just as Paul is not boasting about his suffering more than he is the result of that suffering, so also God is not pleased with holding back favor as much as He is fully pleased with the result of withholding what we miserable and pitiful sons and daughters of God (6:17) are fully assured we need.

Therefore most gladly I will rather boast in my infirmities, that the power of Christ may rest upon me. 10 Therefore I take pleasure in infirmities, in reproaches, in needs, in persecutions, in distresses, for Christ's sake. For when I am weak, then I am strong.
Why is Paul strong? Because he has the dynamite of Christ. Why do we have such power/dynamite (verse 9)?

---

[65] Yes, even the prayer of Christ for a different route than the "cup" in the Garden of Gethsemane (Matthew 26:36–46). An even greater wonder is that the silence of action precedes the loudness of the Father's voice (Psalm 16:7–11).
The usage of "heareth" in 1 John 5:14–15 (KJV) must have the same sense as it does to each of the seven churches in Revelation 2 and 3, where they are told to "hear" if they have ears. In other words, God hears all things as the omnipresent God and yet hears with intent to action as we pray in His will.

Because of the grace He bestows upon us in not giving us that for which we ask. When I was drowning in doubt all of my teenage years and my heart was distressed over a God who didn't audibly answer my cries, my feelings were hurt, but my heart was calmly assured that He was brewing a mix of strength and grace that would serve me well in Christ's power later in life. Even today we'll sing songs that speak of this reality:

> And I will call upon Your name
> And keep my eyes above the waves
> When oceans rise
> My soul will rest in Your embrace
> For I am Yours and You are mine
>
> Your grace abounds in deepest waters
> Your sovereign hand
> Will be my guide
> Where feet may fail and fear surrounds me
> You've never failed and You won't start now.66

So God is not giddy over your and my suffering as much as He is thrilled concerning the strength that will result when He decides to give us grace instead of relief. This strength (12:10) comes only through grace (12:9), and one who is exalted (12:7) does not need grace. The Christian reality is that the "power of Christ" (12:9 NKJV) is tied in with the strength of his apostle (in this case). Perhaps we can see that we look most like Christ when we suffer in perfect submission to the Father for things for which there

---

66 http://www.azlyrics.com/lyrics/hillsongunited/oceanswhere-feetmayfail.html [accessed 12/27/16].

is no sin of our own to blame. Is there anything more worthy of the accusation of being "a Christian"?

Maybe we should take the time now to realize that Paul, who had the "signs of an apostle" (12:12 NKJV), was not healed. So much for the idea that it is always God's will to heal.[67]

12:14–18
14 Now *for* the third time I am ready to come to you.
You might remember this when you look at 13:1.

And I will not be burdensome to you;
It is good that he is saying this because his letter has been recently quite weighty.

for I do not seek yours, but you. For the children ought not to lay up for the parents, but the parents for the children.
As usual, Paul is seeing himself as a parent in the Lord (1 Corinthians 4:10–14; 2 Corinthians 11:2) and is, as you might see in the next verse, expecting to be typically undervalued as a parent.

Moreover, he continually speaks about how he took nothing from them in 1 Corinthians 9, "working with [his] own hands" (1 Corinthians 4:12 NKJV). Paul is saying, "I am after the prize, which is your souls."

---

[67] He could not heal Timothy (1 Timothy 5:23) when he recommended wine in lieu of healing him, nor Trophimus (2 Timothy 4:20).

15 And I will very gladly spend and be spent for your souls; though the more abundantly I love you, the less I am loved.
Here Paul continues his mourning that he feels so little love reciprocated from this church. Remember when he urges them, earlier in the book, to open their hearts to him (6:11–13)? He tells them, "You … are restricted by your own affections" (6:12 NKJV).

16 But be that *as it may,* I did not burden you. Nevertheless, being crafty, I caught you by cunning!
This is seen in the original work he did among them in Acts 18. Other versions of the Bible say this is not the skill of his original evangelism but his sarcastic quotation of the accusations against him.

17 Did I take advantage of you by any of those whom I sent to you? 18 I urged Titus, and sent our brother with *him.*
That unnamed brother of chapter 8 sent with Titus to help the Corinthian believers prepare their offering.

Did Titus take advantage of you? Did we not walk in the same spirit? Did *we* not *walk* in the same steps?
Paul is being careful to remind the Corinthian believers that he is not interested in misusing them—often, he fears, to the growth-stunting lack of demand from them for his needs (11:7–8).[68]

---

[68] Not to mention the long discourse in 1 Corinthians regarding his independent ministry among them—not requiring their financial assistance, which he deserved (1Corinthians 9).

12:19
Again, do you think that we excuse ourselves to you? We speak before God in Christ.
Paul is again calling on God to bear witness to the truth of what he is saying (as in 11:31).

But *we do* all things, beloved, for your edification.
What a weighty statement!

"Paul, everything you do is for their benefit?"
"Yes, everything I do is for their edification, and I even use my place of authority for their edification" (13:10).
There are two very amazing things in this statement: "all things" and "for [their] edification."
"Now then, Paul, why do you do all things for their edification?"

"Edification" is a noun that has been used eighteen times in the New Testament and is often translated as "building."[69] You can certainly see when you behold a large structure—calling it an "edifice"—that it is a related word to "building." So when Paul says that "we do all things … for your edification" (12:19 NKJV), he is saying "we do all things for your" building, your fortification, your structuring, or your stature.

"Even the gifts of an apostle?" (12:12).

---

[69] "G3619 - *oikodomē* - Strong's Greek Lexicon (KJV)." Blue Letter Bible. Web. 11 Jan, 2017. <https://www.blueletterbible.org//lang/lexicon/lexicon.cfm?Strongs=G3619&t=KJV>.

"Yes, those were not for your amazement. They were to make you a building."

"Even in the way you displayed your sacrifice as a parent to us?" (12:13).

"Yes, that was not for your convenience. It was for you to see what solidity and establishment look like."

The real issue here in our being able to relate this properly is to realize that buildings are inanimate objects and don't show emotion. We don't know if a building is sad or mad or glad. Buildings do, however, show things like "relief" or "health" or "stress."

So Paul does things for the functionality of a structure, not for the fun of the process. That is not to say that joy is not a part of the process, but that is not why Paul does "all things" for the Corinthian believers.

The building or edification of a group of people is not only possibly separate from emotional glee, but also separate from immediate observation.

David McCullough, in his book *The Great Bridge*, relays the words of the chief engineer of the Brooklyn Bridge project:

> To such of the general public as might imagine that no work had been done on the New York tower, because they see no evidence of it above the water, I should simply remark that the amount of masonry and concrete

laid on that foundation during the past winter, under water, is equal in quantity to the entire masonry of the Brooklyn tower visible today above the waterline.[70]

The desired product of the body of believers and separated from us due to malady or employment is that we become strong in our callings and in our identity and that we become suitable to house the glory of God found within (as developed so well by Paul in chapter 3).

12:20–21
20 For I fear lest …
Let us quickly realize that this apostle had a motive in all of this visiting and instruction and accountability— which he calls "edification" (12:19 NKJV).

13:1–7
This *will be* the third *time* I am coming to you. "By the mouth of two or three witnesses every word shall be established."
Paul is quoting from Deuteronomy 19:15. Usually this is applied in the context of capital punishment. This really should lead the reader to assume that we are about to get into a topic of eternal significance.

4 For though He was crucified in weakness, yet He lives by the power of God. For we also are weak in

---

[70] Gordon MacDonald *Building Below the Waterline, Shoring Up the Foundations of Leadership* (Peabody, MA: Hendrickson, 2011), vii.

Him, but we shall live with Him by the power of God toward you.

"Toward you" in what? "Toward you" in your sin (verse 2).

"Now then, Paul, why do you do all things for their edification? Why do you go to such extents to get here a third time? Why do you put up with seemingly infantile behavior from some of the pockets of believers among the faithful in the Corinthian church?"

"Because I am afraid many of them are not saved."

Read the next verse.

5 Examine

A great, judicial term in light of verse 2

yourselves *as to* whether you are in the faith.

We read in 8:7 about being "in faith" (NKJV), but here we have the quality of being "in the faith." This means, then, that we are not dealing with a particular aspect of trust as in 8:7, but rather a state of being within the faith recognized by a community as a common standard: the faith. Paul wanted these Corinthian believers who were struggling with prolonged sin in an unrepentant state to examine themselves to determine whether they were in their sin or "in the faith." There is, as you might expect, a difference. We know you are saved by faith, but not just any old faith. Rather, the faith. Faith in what? Faith in the gospel (13:4).

2:12-13 Furthermore, when I came to Troas to preach **Christ's gospel**, and a door was opened to me by the Lord, 13 I had no rest in my spirit, because I did not find Titus my brother; but taking my leave of them, I departed for Macedonia.

4:3-4 But even if our **gospel** is veiled, it is veiled to those who are perishing, 4 whose minds the god of this age has blinded, who do not believe, lest the light of **the gospel** of the glory of Christ, who is the image of God, should shine on them.

5:14-15, 17-19 For the love of Christ compels us, because we judge thus: that if **One died for all**, then all died; 15 and He died for all, that those who live should live no longer for themselves, but for Him who died for them and rose again. ... 17 Therefore, if anyone is in Christ, he is a new creation; old things have passed away; behold, all things have become new. 18 Now all things are of God, **who has reconciled us** to Himself through Jesus Christ, and has given us the ministry of reconciliation, 19 that is, that God was in Christ **reconciling the world to Himself**, not imputing their trespasses to them, and has committed to us the word of reconciliation.

8:9 For you know the grace of our Lord Jesus Christ, that though He was rich, yet for your sakes **He became poor**, that you through His poverty might become rich.

10:14-16 For we are not overextending ourselves (as though our authority did not extend to you), for it was to you that we came with the **gospel of Christ**; 15 not boasting of things beyond measure, that is, in other men's labors, but having hope, that as your faith is increased, we shall be greatly enlarged by you in our sphere, 16 to preach the **gospel** in the regions beyond you, and not to boast in another man's sphere of accomplishment.

11:4 For if he who comes preaches another Jesus whom we have not preached, or if you receive a different spirit which you have not received, or **a different gospel** which you have not accepted—you may well put up with it!

Test yourselves. Do you not know yourselves, that Jesus Christ is in you?

In a previous chapter, Paul speaks to them as a "temple of God" (6:16 NKJV). He is saying, "Remember, you are a house for Jesus Christ on earth."

—unless indeed you are disqualified.

Paul is saying, "*Jesus Christ is in you*, and that is why we are making you a fine building. You are not being crafted because it feels good or because it can be observed. You are being edified because you house *Jesus Christ—unless you are* actually *disqualified*."

6 But I trust that you will know that we are not disqualified.

Paul is saying, "Check out our stability. Look at our foundation. See our squared walls and our plum stature, and you will find that *we are not disqualified*." He even goes on in verse 7 to say that his motive is not that he would look like a proper house for Jesus Christ, but that they would simply do what's right. If they do what's right, that is far more important to him than his validation as a true apostle and agent of Christ in their eyes.

APPENDIX A

Implementing Church Discipline

1. *Make Discipline a Regular Item in All Business Meetings*

   That is, it should be understood that each members' meeting will have the possibility and even the probability that there are those who will need to be discussed for prayer, follow-up, and possible dismissal. After church discipline is a normal part of the church's proceedings, it will seem less and less awkward to carry on such business.

2. *Quit Using Matthew 18:15–20 as a Catch-All Proof Text*

   Why would one use this private-approach idea (of Matthew 18) when it is a public transgression against the testimony of the church? Why would a church assume that you must go through multistage restoration for any and all issues? Did not Paul make a judgment with a separate process in 1 Corinthians 5? Therefore, this careless citation of Matthew 18 must be curtailed, and approaching transgressors must take on various, case-specific, Spirit-led facets and methods. With several echelons of expectation for members, there are inherent safeties which allow for attempts at reconciliation with the church, beginning with the Sunday School teacher. That is to say, each member knows from the time he or she joins that there is to be a committed attendance in both the Lord's Day Bible study and in the weekly body life.

3. *Determine the Readmission Steps of a Repentant Saint*
If the reason church discipline is to occur is for sinners to repent and to prove their relationship with Christ, then it must be expected that some will repent. The church would need to decide whether they would require the same steps as when the believer first joined the particular assembly. This would lead to another vote for admission.

4. *Accountability Body*
Those hitherto mentioned at each echelon in the watchcare and restoration process should be reporting to a body of elders who can offer advice and confirmation of future inquiries involving the timeline of the restoration process.

Conclusion

The exclusion of church members from the body is not particularly pleasant, but it is required—based on 1 Corinthians 5:7, Romans 16:17, 2 Thessalonians 3:10, and a host of other passages—to keep the body clean and right before God.

APPENDIX B

The Corinthian Perspective on the Gospel: 1 Corinthians 9:12–27

9:12
If others are partakers of *this* right over you, *are* we not even more?
Nevertheless, we have not used this right, but endure all things lest we hinder the gospel of Christ.

Paul is saying, "If you knew what I put up with so that my message would be well received and well understood, it would shock you."

This kind of endurance and patience wasn't exercised out of a desire to be hip or relevant or liked or loved in and of itself. This was not a desire to "show the love of Jesus" or to "meet needs." This was for the sake of a message that must be voiced and must be preached.

9:13–14

Do you not know that those who minister the holy things eat of the things of the temple, and those who serve at the altar partake of the offerings of the altar? 14 Even so the Lord has commanded that those who preach the gospel should live from the gospel.

This is not a message on giving, but it is a sub point of Paul's that he is making about the way that people who preach God's truth, particularly evangelistic truth, should be supported physically and fiscally just as the priest was in the temple, the farmer is in his garden (9:3–7), and the ox is under his plow and in his own furrow (9:8–9).

9:15–16

But I have used none of these things, nor have I written these things that it should be done so to me; for it would be better for me to die than that anyone should make my boasting void. 16 For if I preach the gospel, I have nothing to boast of, for necessity is laid upon me; yes, woe is me if I do not preach the gospel!

This is not an unholy boast like Paul speaks about in Ephesians 2:8–9. This is a very holy boasting where one has an "exulting"—or an internal, bursting exuberance—over something that is wonderful and heaven-sent. Paul further explains this elsewhere (Galatians 6:14). It is as if he says, "I get to preach the gospel to everyone all the time without asking them for a thing!"

Having said all that we have said about his right to be supported, Paul was ecstatic that though he was entitled to this privilege, he didn't require their goods or anybody else's for that matter. To freely give a gospel of freedom to every man, bond or free, brought him liberating ecstasy, and he wasn't willing to forfeit that joy simply to capitalize on his rights. Let's see this again in verses 17–18.

9:17–18
For if I do this willingly, I have a reward; but if against my will, I have been entrusted with a stewardship. 18. What is my reward then? That when I preach the gospel, I may present the gospel of Christ without charge, that I may not abuse my authority in the gospel.
Again, it is not always appropriate to lay down one's rights of protection or privilege or provision, but sometimes—for the gospel's sake—not only is it appropriate to do so, but it is also absurd not to do so.

In these verses of 1 Corinthians 9—really, all of them—we find Paul saying, "For those eighteen months that I preached the gospel to you and showed you all of its ramifications, God's justice, God's love, God's scheme of salvation, God's Son and His surrender to His Father, God's forgiveness, God's expectations of gratitude, God's power displayed in life's darkness, I required nothing of you. In fact, I surrendered everything that belonged to me for you, Jews and Gentiles alike."

9:19–22
save some.
Paul is busy seeking others' privilege. Notice how he expects to save souls. Now, I've heard people say, "Well, brother, it's the Lord who does the saving," but 9:22 here is not an exceptional case. It is the norm for Paul, the fellow laborer of God (3:9).

by all means

How casual does this sound? How much of an after-thought does this resemble? How much of the dregs of Paul's schedule do we think this took? Some say that giving of our money to the Lord is marked by setting a giving goal and adjusting the lifestyle around it. Well, it is the same way with time, particularly gospel-sowing, world-evangelizing usage of our time. We set our priorities correctly towards the heart of God in the souls of men, and we adjust our lifestyles around it.

9:23–27
Now this I do for the gospel's sake, that I may be partaker of it with *you*.
24. Do you not know that those who run in a race all run, but one receives the prize? Run in such a way that you may obtain *it*. 25. And everyone who competes *for the prize* is temperate in all things. Now they *do it* to obtain a perishable crown, but we *for* an imperishable crown. 26. Therefore I run thus: not with uncertainty. Thus I fight: not as *one who* beats the air.

Notice the expectation Paul has of striving for an award. It is much like Jesus' (Matthew 6:20). It seems fitting here to remind the reader that we aren't speaking about a nebulous motivation; it's for the gospel. So this striving for a reward as a "runner" is, in the context, the surrendering of rights and the desire for service resulting from being driven by the gospel. Of course, this can only be accomplished by folks who are being saved by the gospel (1 Corinthians 15:1–10).

27. But I discipline my body and bring *it* into subjection, lest, when I have preached to others, I myself should become disqualified.

This sacrifice for the gospel in the life of the seeker or the application of the gospel in the life of the new believer is absolutely discredited with a lack of discipline. This can show itself in a waning focus or with a fleshly or loose lifestyle. We know the gospel doesn't drive us to be loose with our tongues or flippant with our appearance or careless in our holiness. A gracious God drives us to be gracious, yes; a merciful God drives us to be merciful, yes; a loving God drives us to be compassionate, yes; but a Holy God drives us to be fearlessly holy.

A Cross-Culture Church-Planting Strategy[71]

Introduction: The Essential Picture of Church Planting

Before one can have a real appreciation for a method of cross-cultural church planting, one must first come to an understanding of what "church planting" really means. Church planting is the action of stabilizing a new church. Furthermore, a "church" is an assembly. The word behind "church" is *ekklesia* and is found 118 times in the Greek New Testament, and it is translated "church" 115 of those times in the King James Version of the Bible (KJV).[72] A

---

[71] Originally submitted to Dr. C. Thomas Wright by W. J. Sturm in 2012 to LBTS for course ICST 650.
[72] Blue Letter Bible. "Dictionary and Word Search for *ekklēsia (Strong's 1577)*." Blue Letter Bible. 1996–2011. 24 Jun 2011. ≤

survey of the other three times in Acts 19 will show the reader that this was a word used for a gathering of people for the conducting of certain business.

"The essential theme of the whole Bible from beginning to end is that God's historical purpose is to call out a people for himself; that this people is a 'holy' people, set apart from the world...."[73] So the churches, found in various locations, are miniature illustrations of both the calling out that takes place to the people of God at salvation and the calling out that will take place at the second coming when those "in Christ" both "rise" and are "caught up" (1 Thessalonians 4:13–17).

The Need for the Harvest's Lord

The believer who is hopeful of any success on another field should consider that foreign missions is God's work and prayer is, no doubt, the "prepping of the beaches"[74] before the assault of the foot soldier. Marshall speaks of this necessity when he cites a young Williams College student in 1806 by the name of Samuel Mills:

> He and four of his friends were walking through the countryside when a sudden thunderstorm drove them to seek shelter in a large haystack. Held captive by the rain,

---

http:// www.blueletterbible.org/lang/lexicon/lexicon.cfm?Strongs=G1577&t=KJV >

[73] John R. W. Stott. *The Message of the Sermon on the Mount* (Downers Grove, Ill: Inter-Varsity, 1978), 17.

[74] This is a term which speaks to the usage of battleships and bombers to condition the enemies' land before the amphibious assault comes ashore.

> they fell to talking about the 'moral darkness of Asia,'
> when one of them suggested that they pray for that con-
> tinent. One prayer led to another, and the more they
> prayed and talked, the more they became seized with the
> desire to go to Asia as missionaries[75]

Here's an example of what one finds in Matthew 9:38 when the disciples are instructed to pray for laborers to be sent. The next two verses show the reader that these "sent ones" (apostles) were the answer to their own prayer. Two years after these prayer meetings began, a missionary society was formed, and within the next two years, five missionaries were sent to the continent.

Walking the Land

Marshall recorded Mills's later exploits in New England, where he and a colleague searched the states on a two-year fact-finding tour. They were dispatched by two states' missionary societies and traveled down the Mississippi with General Andrew Jackson and his troops. They deter- mined the population-to-minister ratios in each region (or county).[76] Certainly there is a time and place for surveying the mission field for the gospel. While many believers will acknowledge the strategic structure of the spirit world[77]

---

[75] Peter Marshall & David Manuel. *From Sea to Shining Sea* (Old Tappan, NJ: Fleming H. Revell Company, 1986), 120.
[76] Ibid., 122.
[77] Ephesians 6:12 speaks of four different types of non-"flesh and blood" foes (NKJV).

and the placement of these echelons over particular regions of the world,[78] they are reticent to accept the reality
that believers should likewise be strategic. There is no
guarantee that strategists can determine the next place of
God's direction in the missionary's life, but they may
have a place to start, nonetheless.

The Necessity of a Clear Message

Church planting is pointless without the clear message of
the gospel. The church is not merely a clearinghouse for
social programs, nor is it a place where disoriented congregants can find a sense of belonging through
inspirational speeches. J. Mack Stiles captures this well:

> The healthy evangelist is asking ... questions and looking
> for answers so as to guard the gospel. Here is the critical
> test. Could you have preached that sermon if Christ had
> not died on the cross? Could you have developed that
> Christian leadership principle [or whatever principle
> you are sharing] had Christ not been crucified?[79]

This is not to say that cups of "cold water" (Matthew
10:42) are not intended for the lost world but rather that
these acts of kindness have the gospel as their intended
end. James 1:27 speaks of caring for the widow and or-
phan, but it is in the context of having "the faith of our

---

[78] Ezekiel 28:12 and Daniel 10:13 speak of the "king of Tyre" and
"prince of ... Persia" (NKJV), and they are clearly not human beings of whom the prophets speak.
[79] J. Mack Stiles. *Marks of the Messenger* (Downers Grove, Ill: IVP
Books, 2010), 41.

Lord Jesus Christ" (James 2:1 NKJV) and professing this faith with adorning works (James 2:18).

Stiles relays the story of a certain missionary to Guatemala who introduced new dietary ideas and farming ingenuity to the populace. After earning an amount of expertise authority, he was able to share the gospel, and men started to get saved. They stopped getting drunk, beating their wives, and misusing their children. Even the mayor of that town noticed that there was real change.[80]

Why was this? The gospel changes hearts through regeneration and appeals to the mind through the example of the Christ, who died for others' betterment after living years of Spirit-filled, selfless service.

A Clear Message: Not Cultural Reformation

Do sinners act sinful? This is not an issue of making other cultures act more American, more Baptist, more Western, etc.; "church planting" is not about making sinners act saintly.

> Jesus did not command us to change the world. As a matter of fact, it is evident from many passages that He did expect the exact opposite. We are not to expect lost, pagan, secular culture to act and think like Bible-believers.... Churches are appointed agencies for the salvation of men.[81]

---

[80] Ibid., 64.
[81] James A. Alter & Dolton W. Robertson II. *Why Baptist? The Significance of Baptist Principles in an Ecumenical Age* (Sidney, OH: Ancient Baptist Press, 2008), 207.

If an entire culture is made more like the culture of the missionary, the only thing that is guaranteed is that a sort of civilizing has been done. Only those who have bloated, nationalistic ideals of "right" and "ethical" can assume their way is righteous and good before God.

A Clear Message: The Life Commitment

In the spirit of 1 Thessalonians 2:8, a commitment to the conveyance of truth should entail a commitment to invest one's life in some form. It would have been preposterous to tell the apostle that since he had planted the church and left it to the others to lead, he was no longer under expectation before God to lead or account for the development of those who made up that assembly. Acts 16:5 records Paul and Silas as they survey the spiritual health of those churches already planted on preceding trips.[82]

The disbanding of authority (Psalm 2:3), all in the name of the "spirit ... of disobedience" (Ephesians 2:2 NKJV), appears to be much more than a desire for autonomy. This desire for independence has become an idol and has severely crippled much church planting today. All that is being sought is an organized methodology supervised by those who could be considered fathers of a particular church's faith. In angst over Roman Catholicism, many have forgotten the paternal language of the apostle over his churches (1 Corinthians 4:15; 2 Corinthians 11:1–2).

---

[82] David J. Hasselgrave. *Planting Churches Cross-Culturally (Second Edition): North America and Beyond* (Grand Rapids: Baker Books, 2005), 23.

Church-Planting Methodology[83]

Methodology: Commissioning

This is the sending out from the church to plant a church. This commission was given by Jesus Christ, the head of the church (Matthew 28:19–20; Ephesians 1:22–23). Going forward to Acts 13, the reader will notice that both the church body and the Holy Spirit are given credit for sending forth Paul and Barnabas.

Research is a key to determining the place (humanly speaking). With so many places that would make good places, there are countless locations and myriads of subcultures and people groups. There are lost people everywhere, and the need is overwhelming without a location that seems right to Christ through His church.

> In any community it is important to find the most strategic location for building and evangelizing. Find out in which direction the city is growing, residentially. If at all possible, secure property in that direction. The Chamber of Commerce, realtors, and developers can help you determine growth factors of a city.[84]

Of course, this is not to say that the church planter should buy property first. However, the church planter should most certainly use factors like this in determining

---

[83] Ibid., 112.

[84] Sumner C. Wemp. *The Guide to Practical Pastoring* (Shelbyville, TN: Bible & Literature Missionary Foundation, 1982), 53.

where to buy or rent a home for his family among the people group he is considering.

Methodology: Audience Contact

After the missionary is sent out, he must make contact with the people group to whom he is sent. Paul gives the believer some guidance in 1 Corinthians 9:19–22 when he says, "While working with Jews, I live like a Jew, but when working with Gentiles, I live like a Gentile, becoming all things to all men that I may save some of them by whatever means are possible." This guidance tells the believer to, within the bounds of righteousness, blend in with the culture within which he or she seeks to make disciples. It cannot be emphasized enough that the missionary is not to impose his culture[85] on others.[86]

Methodology: Gospel Communication

This is, of course, the objective of going. The gospel, as communicated by the apostle Paul, is the death of Christ for our sins and His resurrection (1 Corinthians 15:1–4).

---

[85] Charles H. Kraft. "Culture, Worldview and Contextualization," *Perspectives on the World Christian Movement: 4th Edition.* Eds., Ralph D. Winter and Steven C. Hawthorne (Pasadena: William Carey Library, 2009), 401; Kraft defines "culture" as the label given by anthropologists to the structured customs and underlying worldview assumptions which govern people's lives. Worldview is included in culture as the deepest level of presuppositions upon which people base their lives.

[86] Ibid., 400.

When a person believes on that truth for his eternal security, he is saved. Church planting—the process of organizing and establishing assemblies of believers—is pointless if there is nothing to believe.

There are, however, little previews of the gospel with the lives of those who have "died" to the old man and are living examples of resurrection power. Romans 6:6–8 speaks of those who "died with Christ" (NKJV), and Romans 6:11 speaks of the new life made possible, yea probable, by the gospel. In other words, the believer preaches the gospel when he can loudly say, "Christ lives in me"! as Paul did (Galatians 2:20 NKJV). "Such a realization will mean that wherever they may be over the course of a given day or week they really do represent Jesus Christ as his appointed ambassadors."[87] So it is with every believer who "walk[s] in the Spirit" (Galatians 5:16 NKJV)—the same "Spirit" who testifies of Christ (John 15:26). One must not be quick to overlook the depth of this step. Hiebert points this out:

> Before missionaries go to another country for the first time, they often think of the great distance they must travel to get to their field of labor. But once they arrive on the field, the greatest problem to be faced is in the last few feet. What a shock! The missionary has studied for many years. He has traveled thousands of miles to communicate the gospel of Christ. He now stands face-to-face

---

[87] J.I. Packer & Gary A. Parrett. *Grounded in the gospel: Building Believers the Old-Fashioned Way* (Grand Rapids: Baker Books, 2010), 169.

with the people of his respondent culture and he is unable to communicate the most simple message![88]

Perhaps the largest issue with sharing the life-changing message of the gospel is actually "decoding the Biblical message" [89] and "encoding"[90] it back into the culture wherein the missionary has been sent.

Methodology: Congregating Believers

Of course, this is a critical time when we help those who are converted to understand the necessity of community life—building a group of converts around the idea of the conveyance of truth, the care for others, and the corporate worship of Christ. The consistent example of the shepherd in the lives of his specific people group is essential. This means he must have a measure of sanctified stubbornness. We may stay even without a salary for an amount of time. The apostle Paul knew this well. He continually reminded the church at Thessalonica that he provided for his own needs in their situations.[91] This probably allowed him to,

---

[88] Hesselgrave, 426.

[89] Ibid., 427.

[90] Ibid., 428.

[91] Bruce Steffes & Michelle Steffes. *Your Mission: Get Ready! Get Set! Go!* (Linden, NC: Dr. Bruce Steffes, 2010), 14–15; Steffes reminds the reader that "we are so used to the truth that Paul had a tent-making career in Corinth that we forget that Christians other than those in Corinth helped him financially and in other ways. He did receive assistance from other individuals and churches. In Romans 15:24, the original language was clear that he was talking about money when he wrote and asked for support." However, from

through the collective actions of these congregations, meet many other needs of both the saints in Jerusalem and fellow church planters.[92]

The number of congregants is not nearly as critical as the reality that some are congregating and that they are beginning to appreciate eternal things, such as the purpose their new Savior and King has given them in the spreading of truth through multiple like-minded (anchored in the one truth), heaven-conscious assemblies of believers. This will mean that truth—not programs—will need to be paramount.

If a pastor is to disseminate truth to groups of believers, preaching patiently the whole counsel of God, then a pastor can expect this process to take at least three years.[93] This love of truth and this joy of leading God's sheep beside still waters is not a quick process.

Methodology: Leadership Consecration

Leaders must be led. Hudson Taylor knew what it was to live by faith. This faith was observed by others through the generous sharing of that which he had. He was challenged by Scripture in front of those to whom he wished to minister, and he, like those of his future flock, was faced with whether he would trust the truth.[94] Leaders will

---

the viewpoint of the Corinthians and Thessalonians, Paul was supported by those other than themselves.

[92] Dennis W. Bickers. *The Tentmaking Pastor: The Joy of Bivocational Ministry* (Grand Rapids: Baker Books, 2000), 10.

[93] Ibid., 15.

[94] Phyllis Thompson. *Hudson Taylor: God's Venturer* (Chicago: Moody Press, _____), 10.

lead as they are led. Those whom God appears to be setting aside for the work of the gospel will be challenged to live by faith as they see it exhibited before them. Those leaders who are being considered to carry on the work will be faced with whether they wish to lead a typical American way of life or whether the main thing in their life is the dissemination of truth through God's assemblies.

Part of this faith will need to be cultivated in prayer. That is, it takes faith to pray—faith in the Scriptures, that is. It also takes faith to keep praying. Is God able? Is God willing to fund and fuel His own program of multiplying assemblies? One thing is certain: if the church planter is not praying powerfully before he begins, he may find it difficult to get much done in the field.[95] Whether in finances or in the area of the changing of hearts, Hudson Taylor exhibited the power of God through prayer in England before departing for China. This was a faith that he would later teach through example to those first-generation converts in his target people group.[96]

Culture Shock

The world is not American. America is not even uni-cultural. There are subcultures within America's culture. It will take the grace of God in the planning stages to be fully prepared and in the actual mission work to be fully engaged while, in the planter's humanness, he may feel out of place.

---

[95] Ibid., 16.
[96] Ibid., 43.

> You can only hope and pray that you are not too misera-
> ble while you grow through it and that it does not leave
> you scarred. Even if you survive relatively unscathed,
> you will see those on your ... mission trip who are having
> a really rough time—and the most affected may even be
> the career missionaries you are going to work with.[97]

It seems fitting, then, to say that it is an unreal expectation to feel right at home upon immediate integration
with another culture. Taking the task a day at a time with
a lifetime perspective seems to be the best approach. The
marriage partner is doubtless the best partner one can have
in the work of the Lord. Metering the stress in your spouse
is of utmost importance.[98] Perhaps the most refreshing
thing about church planting is that there is no scriptural
directive for how long it is supposed to take place. Speed
up and slow down as God gives grace.

---

[97] Steffes & Steffes, 186.
[98] Ibid., 189.

APPENDIX C

The Corinthian Perspective on Baptism

Turn to Acts 18:1–8 and let me just say in passing that if you will observe this passage where it lies in the book of Acts, a couple of things become obvious:

1. This was Paul's missionary journey.
2. Baptism already had an understanding of requiring "much water" (Eunuch, Acts 8).

It seems there are some other things we learn from this record of the first trip to Corinth:

1. Jesus was declared in the town already. As a matter of fact, He was declared near the synagogue (Acts 18:5–7).
2. Baptism was more than a Jewish thing—or else the ruler of the synagogue wouldn't have bothered with it (Acts 18:8).

3. When the head of a house got saved, got baptized, and feared God, typically the whole house followed suit (Acts 18:8).
4. Baptism was not private but, rather, public and caused many problems (Acts 18:9–15). Why? It's what Christians do!
5. This was followed up with an expectation that a new way of life had begun, and this new way of life continued with worship and instruction with the church (Acts 18:11, 17). Why? It's what Christians do!

Now, let's go to the second letter Paul wrote[99] to the Corinthians, which we call "First Corinthians," and let's find more information about the baptism and the believers at Corinth. There are a few things that are still glaringly evident:

1. Some time has passed.
    a. This is the second letter since they became Christians (1 Corinthians 5:9).
    b. They had enough believers to have some factions (1 Corinthians 1:11–14).
2. The formula being stated as one is baptized is not as important as the intent behind the baptism (1 Corinthians 1:12–14).
3. Baptism is not part of the gospel (1 Corinthians 1:17).

---

[99] Apparently, he wrote another letter (1 Corinthians 5:9).

Now that we have reviewed all of this, let us consider that baptism is found two other times in this book. One of them is in verse 29 of chapter 15 and describes a certain group of people who were baptized on behalf of dead folks. The other time it's found is in chapter 12, verses 12–13.

What is evident is that Paul—having used "baptism" only in relation to water in this letter so far, and only as "water baptism" in that zany idea later in the book, and not bringing it up again in the second letter—is comparing water baptism to this "baptism of the spirit" by using the word "baptism." If that's true, if water baptism is to picture spirit baptism, then:

1. What is true about spirit baptism, which takes place for every believer, is pictured by water.
2. It is to be the beginning to life with the body of Christ (with the obvious relevance to a "local body").
   a. Paul is not talking to people who never meet.
   b. Paul is not talking to people in separate towns.
   c. Paul is not talking to people in different churches.
   d. Paul is not talking to people who believe different things.
   e. No, Paul is talking to a single group of people in a single house-church in a single

town who always meet in worship and discipleship, and he is saying to them, "You are the body."

3. It is to acknowledge that the individual believer, as one of many being likewise water baptized, belongs to that body. No preacher should ever baptize somebody if he or she is not going to be a part of the body he is shepherding.

   a. You are needed (1 Corinthians 12:4–11).
   b. You need others in your church.

Conclusion

1. Baptism is immersion.
2. Baptism is for all believers.
3. All believers are to be in a local church and thus baptized publicly.
4. When one says, "I wish to be baptized," he or she is saying, "I have been washed by the Spirit of God because I have believed the gospel of Jesus, and I submit to my Lord's requirement to be a faithful, thriving part of the believers here at this assembly."

APPENDIX D

The Corinthian Perspective on the Lord's Supper: Betrayed, Broken, and Bleeding (1 Corinthians 11:17–34)

1. These Corinthian believers could be described as *regularly meeting* (11:17, 18, 20, 33, 34).
   a. Consider that it was something they were assumed to be doing for worship in 14:23, 26.
   b. It was something they did for giving/collecting resources in 16:1.
2. These Corinthian believers were *regularly divided.*
   a. This was a blessing (11:19).
   b. We would not even have this great discourse if he were not fussing at a church (11:17).
   c. These believers were *regularly celebrating.* (11:26).
   d. A celebration of His death.

    e. The originals speak of a "lauding" rather than a simple "demonstration."

    f. As we celebrate this Supper, we are asking people to be happy about a death. The Lord's Supper is a celebration that the Lord Who was betrayed and broken and bleeding is yet alive.

    g. Both components are that of celebration.

    h. The gospel is what saves us (1:21, 15:1–4).

    i. The Resurrection is part of this gospel because it assures us that His death was special and valid.

3. These were *regularly mourning* (11:27–34), guilty in not respecting or acknowledging the body (11:29).[100]

    a. This makes sense in light of the context carrying through 12:31.[101]

    b. Can you think of a worse way not to discern the Lord's body than to withhold love (chapter 13)?

Conclusion

If the body of those who regularly meet together (11:17) and work together (12:15ff) is being addressed, then the body of Christ at Corinth is to partake of the Lord's Supper together.

---

[100] Some have said this "body" of verse 29 is speaking of the "body of Christ" in the bread, but the lack of parallelism in the "cup" not being a damning thing tells us that it is not referring to the flesh of Christ.

[101] The love chapter (chapter 13) then makes sense in light of the horrible things done to one another in the Lord's Supper then carried forth into a discourse on the body.

1. We have no authority from Scripture to presume other circumstances (such as "anybody can partake" or even "any Christian can partake").
2. We do have authority to assume the case as it is found here: Local churches celebrate the Lord's Supper together (churches are made up of those who are saved, baptized, and covenanted or committed together with one another).
3. We also want to remember that regularity is what the Scripture writers were after, not rote regulation.

A Biblical and Logical Case for Closed Communion[102]

Let us now present a biblical and logical argument for local church "closed communion," manifesting itself in a "members only" meeting to partake of the body and blood of Christ. Unwittingly, those who argue for the "close communion" of yesteryear—often calling it "closed communion"—have argued best for a local church-exclusive Lord's Table.

It seems that now would be a good time to define the term "closed communion" as "the practice among Baptists in which they limit the participation in the observance of the Lord's Supper, to those who are members in good

---

[102] A paper originally submitted to Liberty Baptist Theological Seminary in Lynchburg, VA, in completion of the class THEO 620 (Ecclesiology) for the ThM in October 2014.

standing in Baptist churches."[103] It needs to be even more concise as saying "those who are members in good standing in a particular church." This membership taking part in the Lord's Supper begins with a public committal through identification with Christ through "the immersion of [professing believers]."[104]

"Closed communion," then, used to be simply an admission of converted and immersed church members to the Lord's Table. The old "closed communion" is what this paper will label "close communion" while "closed communion" will limit the Lord's Supper to those who are converted, immersed, and a part of the particular Baptist church that is conducting the Lord's Supper. Probably the reason historical peoples would not have made this distinction is because of the presence of Baptist churches in minimal fashion—perhaps one per town. Consider those coming before:

> During the years from 1749 to 1756 Backus wrestled with several issues.... Backus adopted an antipaedobaptist position and was himself baptized in 1751. Between 1753 and 1755, as the leader of the antipaedobaptist Separates, Backus experimented with open communion, at times in bitter debate with members of his congregation about the acceptability of members who favoured infant baptism. Unable to achieve exemption from the religious tax as Separates and divided from the rest of the Middleborough church over communion, Backus and his

---

[103] O. L. Hailey, *Why Close Communion and Not Open Communion* (Roger Williams Heritage Archives, 1899), 195.

[104] Thomas R. Schreiner and Matthew R. Crawford *The Lord's Supper: Remembering and Proclaiming Christ Until He Comes* (New American Commentary Studies in Bible & Theology. Nashville, TN: B & H, 2011), 285.

loyal antipaedobaptist following adopted closed communion and antipaedobaptist articles of faith. The new
congregation called itself the 'Baptist Church of Christ in
Middleborough, Bridgewater, and Raynham.[105]

Clearly, there was but one Baptist church in Middleborough, Bridgewater, and Raynham, so what is now
termed "close communion" was for all practical purposes
"closed communion." Why? All converted, immersed
church members had only one church to attend. Therefore,
to limit the participants of the Lord's Table to immersed
converts would have been limiting the Lord's Table to that
one and only Baptist Church.

Considerations

A Natural Product of "Regenerate Church Membership"

That is to say, if a church were interested in being sure
that all the members were saved, that would mean that
they, the leaders and congregation, would be taking steps
to know the flock themselves. How does it follow, then,
that one would take the chance of allowing another to take
"in an unworthy manner" (1 Corinthians 11:27 NKJV) by
simple ignorance of who that person is and how his or her
soul stands before God? Consider the Separatists:

---

[105] W. H. Brackney, "Backus, Isaac," ed. Timothy Larsen et al., *Bio-graphical Dictionary of Evangelicals* (Leicester, England; Downers Grove, IL: InterVarsity Press, 2003), 27–28.

> A Congregationalist separatist movement especially
> prominent in New England during the period 1735–
> 1750. The Separates were strict Congregationalists who
> desired to return to the original New England ideals of
> the seventeenth century.... Separate congregations over-
> turned the traditional New England parish system and
> challenged the practice of supporting the clergy with
> public taxation. Reviving the call for visible sainthood,
> they demanded that candidates for church membership
> show the marks of true conversion before being admit-
> ted. Consequently, they adopted the practice of closed
> Communion....[106]

This "parish system" had one church per geography. It follows, then, that every perceived convert who was worthy of the Lord's Supper was a part of that particular church. Consider another example: the General Synod of the Associate Reformed Presbyterian Church (GSARPC), a small Presbyterian denomination, which "grew to establish four synods by 1803, and in 1804 the first general synod was formed. Controversies over exclusive psalm-singing, closed Communion and church government led eventually to synodical [exercise]."[107] There would not have been non-GSARPC members taking part in communion.

Since there were not multiple congregations in specific geographies, it follows that only those of the particular church would be allowed at the Lord's Table. It would have been unfathomable that a pastor would labor over his membership to be sure they were converted only to allow

---

[106] Daniel G. Reid et al., "Separatists," *Dictionary of Christianity in America* (Downers Grove, IL: InterVarsity Press, 1990).
[107] Reid, "Congregationalists."

one in from another flock—and that's the best-case scenario for a visitor in the midst. This, then, is magnified when one considers endangering his own flock with the judgment of God. Surely the argument of 1 Corinthians 5 and putting one on the outside so that God judges him or her (1 Corinthians 5:13) speaks to this outrageous notion that you could be admitting leaven into your flock in time to partake of the Passover of God (1 Corinthians 5:6–11).

A Natural Product of "Immersionism"

There was a time when the local church was of such paramount importance to Baptists that the mode of baptism would be examined. Even more than that, the credentials of the church that baptized them would be examined to see if the baptism was valid.

Imagine going to this extreme to see that candidates could be members of your church only to exercise anything other than closed communion! Why the rigid investigation of a member only to allow any member of any supposed immersionist church to take part in your own church's Lord's Supper? To go to such investigative lengths to be sure a given person is qualified to receive baptism, only to admit one to the table who has not been so examined, minimizes the gravity with which the ordinances are to be observed. Consider the Primitive Baptists:

> Most Primitive Baptists oppose church auxiliaries not found in Scripture, such as Bible/tract societies, seminaries and Sunday schools. Their churches group only in associations which meet annually and correspond with

each other by letter or messenger. Their church order has been characterized by simple, monthly worship meetings, closed communion, refusal to accept members without Primitive Baptist immersion and untrained/un-salaried, bivocational ministers.[108]

The idea of allowing only those whom the pastors and membership have rigorously qualified to be members to take part in the Lord's Supper is logical. If "close communion" allows any baptized member of another church to take part, then "closed communion" assures and reassures that those who pass membership inquiry of an autonomous church are able to partake of the body and blood of Christ. In other words, church membership becomes something for which one is examined but one time with this whole "transfer by letter" or "close communion" mentality.

Now, the author of this paper is not "Landmarkian," but their ecclesiology is worthy of emphasis:

[Landmarkers] question the validity of transferring church membership by letter, a practice common among many Baptist churches but seen as a violation of the rights of the local church by Landmarkers.... Baptisms by immersion not performed under the auspices of a Baptist church were not true baptisms but "alien immersions." Access to the Lord's Supper was protected by the practice of "closed communion," allowing only baptized members of a given local church to participate in its celebration.[109]

---

[108] Reid, "Primitive Baptists."
[109] Reid, "Landmark Baptists."

Truly, strong local-church proponents are protective of the right to approve of their own church members. As such, when the highest authority in the kingdom of God on earth is the local church, even the Lord's Supper participants should be heavily scrutinized by the local church so as to protect the flock from the chastening hand of God.

A Token of Fidelity to One Another

If, in fact, believers are to be unified, and this unification is to be found in the assembling of believers who are found in concert as the audience of the epistles of the great apostles, then there should be tokens of this unification. What are these?

"[Baptism and the Lord's Supper] are significant for a church because they serve as 'oaths of fidelity and obedience' to Christ."[110] Apparently, the "oath of fidelity" is not to be the normative voting in of a new member but rather the worthy partaking of the church ordinances. That is to say, there should be no "oath of fidelity" short of the Lord's Supper and Baptism. If baptism is to be shared with one's local assembly, why would the audience partaking of the Lord's Supper be anybody other than the members of that assembly?

> He who is not baptized, and therefore not a member of the church, cannot renew her or his unity with or commitment to the body. For this reason, some strict

---

[110] R. Stanton Norman, *The Baptist Way: Distinctives of a Baptist Church* (Nashville, TN: Broadman & Holman Publishers, 2005), 155.

communionists limit communion to the members of the specific church in which the ordinance is celebrated.... I even have some misgivings about extending transient communion to visiting members of other Baptist churches....[111]

All of this says that membership has its privileges. If a person has not taken the steps to be a member, why would there then be an assumption that he or she is right with God in the first place?

Certainly no one would have thought of partaking of the Lord's Supper without having made full profession of his conversion to Christ. Most Christian churches, throughout the entire Christian era, have not only understood the New Testament practice thus, but have themselves practiced close communion, *i.e.*, have regarded communion as an ordinance to be participated in only by those who have fulfilled all the conditions of church-membership.[112]

If the membership has been carefully vetted through the membership process, how could something that succeeds this commitment and vetting process not include this very same group and others who have not been so vetted? It seems, then, that only those who have passed the test of membership would pass the test of the Lord's Table.

[111] John Hammett, *Biblical Foundations for Baptist Churches: A Contemporary Ecclesiology* (Grand Rapids, MI: Kregel, 2005), 285–287.
[112] C. A. Jenkens, *Baptist Doctrines* (Roger Williams Heritage Archives, 1890), 270.

No Foreign Members or Body Parts Herein

Few would argue that the passages regarding the "body of Christ" refer to the church as it is explicit in passages like Ephesians 1:21–23. However, the word "church" is used in at least four senses in current Christianity. In English-speaking Christianity, the most prolific use is that of referring to a "church building." Perhaps a discussion on the word *ekklesia* is in order, but it suffices simply to point out that it has a biblical usage of "ones called out to assemble." This is often used of the "church universal," where all who are born again are considered as those who are assembled in Christ (Ephesians 1:10).

Then the word is used in reference to the local church—a group of people who really do assemble on a regular basis. It is this "church" to which the Pauline epistles, by and large, are written.

Lastly, there is this notion of the "corporate church," which is a term used for all true local churches in a general fashion. Now that this foundation is laid, consider the following words:

> One of the main points of the Apostle's earnest admonitions in I. Cor., xi., is that the Supper is not a social ordinance, in which a few might join as a social repast, but that they should wait one for another; and with the whole church assembled, they should partake of the Supper. Again, he declares, "For we being many, are one

bread and one body; for we are all partakers of that one bread." I. Cor. x. 17.[113]

If, in fact, the "church" is the "body of Christ" as spoken above, it seems like the passage cited above should be taken strictly in the sense that the audience would have understood it. There is little or no biblical evidence that there was more than one local church in Corinth. The opening verses of each of the epistles to the Corinthians make it abundantly clear that they were written to that one church. It is the natural understanding, then, of these "body of Christ" passages that they are, as a "local church," a body of Christ.

This is not to say that there is not a "universal body of Christ" in a corporate sense, but this concept has its natural outworkings in the local consequence of each church. This does not, then, leave room for visitors from other "bodies"—each of which represents the "body of Christ" as a separate autonomous reality.

Pastoral Oversight and Protection of the Flock

The simple concept of "bishop" or "elder" refers to the function and character of the pastor in overseeing, in a mature manner, the fair goings of his sheep. "Do we not owe a duty to our Lord and Master to protect his table? And can we better do it than by inviting to the Lord's Table only those whom we *know* to be his *consistent—that*

---

[113] R. M. Dudley, *Close Communion* (Roger Williams Heritage Archives, 1890), 213.

is, *Scriptural—followers?"*[114] Who would say they are
protecting the flocks without also protecting their ordinances entrusted to them by their Head, Jesus Christ?

Consider how a pastor protects his flock from wolves
according to the spirit of Acts 20 and imagine what authority a pastor has to do so when he cannot limit the
Lord's Table to "members in good standing." People who
have been excused from church membership are not allowed to partake of Communion since that person is by all
appearances an unbeliever. "He must be barred from the
Table."[115] How can a pastor do this without limiting the
Lord's Table to his membership?

The First Evidence of Church Discipline

Jonathan Edwards speaks of not eating with those who
preach divisive doctrines in his sermon "The Nature of
Excommunication" and its exposition of verses like Romans 16:17. Interestingly enough, he insists that the
command to avoid eating with these excommunicants in
2 Thessalonians 3:14 is definitely not speaking about the
Lord's Supper.[116] This seems so foreign to the notion that
one can enjoy the most intimate of signs of devotion to the
gospel with people with whom he or she, according to Edwards, is not even allowed to share a meal. In other words,
you can treat a person "as an heathen man and a publican"

---

[114] Clarence Larkin, *Why I Am a Baptist* (Washington DC: American
Baptist Publication Society, 1902), 44.

[115] Schreiner & Crawford, *The Lord's Supper: Remembering and
Proclaiming Christ Until He Comes*, 379.

[116] Jonathan Edwards, "The Nature of Excommunication," *Free
Grace Broadcaster,* Issue 222 (Winter 2012): 37.

(Matthew 18:17 KJV), but you can still allow him to be a part of your fellowship in the Lord's Supper.

This seems highly improbable. Even less probable is that a pastor would allow people to take part in the Lord's Supper when that pastor is not even assured that they have peace with whatever church of which they claim to have a part. This is highly inconsistent—not to allow those under church discipline to take part in the Lord's Supper, but to allow those who may be a part of a church that does not properly participate in church discipline. Hence, closed communion makes the most fluid sense.

Conclusion

A Warning Concerning Extremism

Perhaps the most pragmatic consideration of whether a church should institute communion "for members only" is whether a church or movement of churches flourishes with this practice. As a matter of fact, "closed" or "exclusive" communion has been a tenant of extremist church movements which have, for the most part, placed themselves into extinction. Consider Reid's summary of "Six-Principle Baptists" as an example:

> During the Interregnum some English Baptists adopted Hebrews 6:1–2 as a six-point confessional standard: repentance, faith, baptism, laying on of hands, the resurrection of the dead and eternal life. Debate arose among General Baptists concerning whether or not this required a new church ordinance: the laying of hands on new converts. John Griffith's *God's Oracle and Christ's Doctrine* (1655) became the definitive defense for

churches affirming this. The Standard Confession (1660) required that new believers submit to the laying on of hands in order to "receive the promise of the Holy Spirit." But because the general assembly refused to adopt the Six Principles as its only official standard, Six-Principle Baptists separated and established their own assembly (1690). Their theology was Arminian, and they practiced closed communion.... By the 1670s several Rhode Island Six-Principle churches had formed what perhaps was the first Baptist association in America. In the 1940s three churches identified as Six-Principle Baptists listed 280 members, living mostly in Rhode Island and Pennsylvania.[117]

In this case, believing that only members should partake of a particular church's Lord's Supper is as seemingly extreme as requiring new converts to have hands laid upon them for the indwelling of the Holy Spirit. The warning, then, remains: Do not adopt this for extremism's sake.

The Answer Remains

Having spoken a caution against extremes, one should remember that doing nothing is an extreme of its own. It is unfortunate that the arguments from Matthew 18 and 1 Corinthians 5:11 will not suffice for many. It is unfortunate that private family meetings are not prioritized in this American, materialized church. Let those who wish to take part in the Lord's Table first prove themselves as capable bearers of the body and blood of Christ to the pastor

---

[117] Reid et al., *Dictionary of Christianity in America.*

through examination and to the church through covenant membership.

APPENDIX E

Spiritual Formation

Perhaps the biggest mistake of today's popular Christianity is that of making spirituality a mere component of some total fitness or wholeness. This almost gives the idea that one can be somewhat emotionally fit for life although he may very well be in poor health spiritually. Even worse, it could be said, "This person is in good emotional and social health, but he could really be much better off if he had a spiritual aspect to his life as well." Believers must be continually challenged with the reality that all actions, all words, and all thoughts are spiritually significant. Westerhoff quotes another as saying there is "no difference between the perfecting of the soul and the business of life."[118]

Defining "Spiritual"

---

[118] John Westerhoff. *Spiritual Life: The Foundation for Preaching and Teaching* (Louisville: Westminster John Knox Press, 1994), 2.

Ephesians 1:3 states that the believer has all of the bless-
ings from the Spirit in Christ. Real spirituality can be
defined in no better way than living the life that comes
from God's Spirit.

Defining "Formation"

"Formation" has the idea of "causing to exist." This along
with the "spirit life" has the idea that God's Spirit is form-
ing real life in a person. The only time in the New
Testament this word is found in this sense is Galatians
4:19. However, it is quite passive. It is much like floating
effortlessly versus swimming.[119] It is not that the individual disciple finally achieves spiritual formation for
himself but rather that Jesus Christ the Master is formed
in the disciple, bringing the life of God. The Spirit of God
performs this formation, and He is committed to it.

The Spirit's Commitment Through the Shepherd

Church leaders need to be careful to allow the Holy Spirit
to do the work that He desires so that the members are "set
… in the body" as He desires (1 Corinthians 12:18
NKJV). Hebrews 2:13 gives the sense that Christ was
given His people from the Father. He took these children
committed to His charge very seriously, and Jesus followed up on disciples whom He believed were given to
Him for oversight (Luke 5; John 21). Moreover, Acts

---

[119] Ibid, 43.

20:28 identifies the Holy Spirit as the One who makes the shepherd-flock connection.

Galatians 6:1–2 speaks of restoration and the bearing of one another's burdens (NKJV). Certainly, these ideas mesh in their application as one can arguably support another's burdens while restoring him. Compassion will drive people in the ministry to give of their time and energy for the well-being of other souls (Luke 10).

Pastoral ministry is most certainly a type of Christian friendship that carries all manner of typical duties that one would expect a pastor to carry out, such as administration, counseling, visitation, weddings, funerals, preaching, teaching, and even coordination of activities. There is a reaching out with help, encouragement, or support to another at a time of need, understood as "empathy" instead of "sympathy" or "investment" instead of "intrigue." No soul in the church will ever feel left alone so long as there is one who cares for their souls (Hebrews 13:17). Spiritual formation finds fruition with the help of God's shepherds.

The Spirit's Commitment Through Discipline

The Holy Ghost set the pastors as "overseers" (Acts 20:28 KJV). As such, if Christ is present in His church through the Holy Spirit during discipline (Matthew 18:20), then it behooves well-meaning churches to discipline their members lovingly (Hebrews 10:22–25). If being part of the body is necessary for the formation of spiritual life, then church discipline—both informal and corrective—is essential to this formation.

The Spirit's Commitment Through the Endowment of Gifts

First Corinthians 12:4–6 gives a treatise on the gifts of the Spirit. He is concerned with the gifts (12:4) while Jesus is concerned with administrations (12:5 KJV) and the Father is concerned with operations (12:6 KJV). These gifts are known as spiritual gifts (12:1) because they are given to the members of the body of Christ by the Holy Spirit at His discretion (12:11).[120] The Holy Spirit of God is given the credit for the assignment of "spiritual gifts" to members of Christ's body.

The discipleship process is incomplete without the exercise of one's spiritual gifts within the church. This means that the individual and the church are dysfunctional and "unformed" without them. If the believer is to be formed by the Spirit, if the believer is to have the life of God formed in him, then the equipment by this same Spirit is foundational to this formation.

The Spirit Commitment of Wisdom

Perhaps one of the most comforting titles of the Holy Spirit comes from Isaiah 11:2, where He is known as the

---

[120] Only believers in Christ as "Lord" are avenues of spirituality in the gifting sense (1 Corinthians 12:3). Every believer in Christ is an avenue of spirituality in the gifting sense (1 Corinthians 12:7). These gifts are listed in this chapter, Romans 12, Ephesians 4, and 1 Peter 4:10. There should be an interest in accumulating these gifts as available vessels (1 Corinthians 12:31). There is a significance regarding the spiritual gifts of the individual at the coming of Christ (1 Corinthians 1:7). Perhaps there will be an accountability of all those who were stewards of these "spiritual gifts."

"Spirit of wisdom" (NKJV). The Holy Spirit forms life in the believer by giving him discernment to know where he is least suited to perform in a life-filled manner. He will also teach the believer what holiness is and give him the power to overcome (2 Corinthians 6:14–7:1, 10:5). Sometimes this means there is an ability to see what is really happening in a seemingly meaningless occurrence.[121]

Conclusion

A life without the life of God is no life at all. Westerhoff calls this an "ever-deepening" walk with God.[122] The Spirit of God, through His indwelling, His pastors, His giftings, His discipline, and His wisdom, is He who forms Christ in us (Galatians 4:19). The yielding of the believer is the ingredient so often missing, and this author finds the formation of Christ in himself one and the same as the formation of the life of God (Colossians 3:4; 1 John 5:20).

---

[121] Ibid, 22.
[122] Ibid, 32.

INDEX

Scripture Index

John
15:26	Appendix B
19:13	5:10
21	Appendix E

Acts
8	Appendix C
9	11:31–33
12:21	5:10
14	11:31–33
16	11:31–33
16:5	Appendix B
18	1:15–18; 12:14–18
18:1–17	Appendix C
18:12	5:10
18:16	5:10
18:17	5:10
19:21	1:15–18
20	8:1–4
20:3	1:15–18
20:7	2:14
20:28	Appendix E
25:6	5:10
25:10	5:10
25:17	5:10
26:15	4:5

Romans
2:15	3:4–6
5	4:6
6:6	5:14b–15a; Appendix B

3:14–16	3:12–17
3:14	4
3:18	3:12–17; 4; 5:5
4	11:23–28
4:1–4	3:12–17
4:1	4; 4:7–5:1
4:2	4; 5:11–12
4:3–6	4; 4:5
4:3–4	13:1–7
4:3	4:5
4:4–6	3:12–17
4:4	4; 5:15b–17
4:6	4; 4:3–4; 5:10; 5:15b–17
4:7–16	3:12–17
4:7	5:6–8
4:14	5:10
4:15	4
4:16–18	3:12–17
4:16	4
4:17	4
5	6:1–2
5:1–8	5:2–4
5:1	5:6–8
5:3	5:15b–17
5:7	5:13–14a
5:10–11	7:1; 10
5:11	4; 7:11–12
5:13–21	6:12–17
5:14–19	13:1–7
5:14–15	7:1
5:14	5:15b–17; 7:11–12; 8:8–9

About the Author

Bill Sturm serves as Senior Pastor at Sandy Ridge Baptist Church of Hickory, NC. Previously, he served as the Associate Pastor of Berean Baptist Church in Fayetteville, NC, following almost nine years on active duty in the United States Army. He also specializes in world religions and church history. His most recent formal education was the completion of his Th.M. from Liberty Baptist Theological Seminary (2014). He currently serves as a Brigade Chaplain in the United States Army Reserve.

Bill was saved out of a life of "Sinner's Prayer"-ism and placed his faith in the finished work of Christ alone in 1999. He has felt the call to ministry most of his life, having preached as a fifth-grader to his peers in children's church. He is a student of Scripture, a student of his family, and a student of people, and enjoys theology, ethics, soccer, animals, music, hunting, fishing, and trains. His greatest challenge is his prayer life. Preaching Christ and His cross is Bill's passion. He is happily married to Nikki, his wife of twenty years, and they have three children— one of whom is married, while another is serving in the U.S. Air Force.

Contact Bill at: pastorbillsrbc@gmail.com.

About Sermon To Book

SermonToBook.com began with a simple belief: that sermons should be touching lives, *not* collecting dust. That's why we turn sermons into high-quality books that are accessible to people all over the globe.

Turning your sermon series into a book exposes more people to God's Word, better equips you for counseling, accelerates future sermon prep, adds credibility to your ministry, and even helps make ends meet during tight times.

John 21:25 tells us that the world itself couldn't contain the books that would be written about the work of Jesus Christ. Our mission is to try anyway. Because in heaven, there will no longer be a need for sermons or books. Our time is now.

If God so leads you, we'd love to work with you on your sermon or sermon series.

Visit www.sermontobook.com to learn more.

www.ingramcontent.com/pod-product-compliance
Lightning Source LLC
Chambersburg PA
CBHW061823040426
42447CB00012B/2781